"Michael is a master of incorporating fiery flavors into everyday and not-s~ cuisine is not a hold-my-beer-and-watch-this style of presentatio~ a true chilihead can appreciate."

—**John Hard,** founder of CaJohn's Fiery

"*The Spicy Food Lovers' Cookbook* is the ultimate culinary experien how to add dimensions of flavor to everyday meals. Michael Hultqui ~, exciting the taste buds with each bold and fiery recipe."

—**Jessica Gavin,** certified culinary scientist and author of *Easy Culinary Science for Better Cooking*

"Spicy food enthusiasts, rejoice! You now have a fiery food playbook dedicated to you. It doesn't matter if you are a novice or an endorphin addict in search of the next hottest dish, Michael has a recipe for you."

—**Al "Buddah" Goldenberg,** founder of I Love It Spicy!

"Mike's passion for all things spicy pops off the page in his newest book, and it's jam-packed with delicious recipes! Whether you like your spice full-force or dialed back a bit, Mike shows you how to bring the heat to your kitchen."

—**April Anderson,** creator of Girl Gone Gourmet and author of *Gourmet Cooking for One or Two*

"*The Spicy Food Lovers' Cookbook* elevates the flavor of both familiar and not-so-familiar dishes with the many varieties of that vegetable of extreme smack—the chili pepper."

—**Kirsten K. Shockey,** author of *Fiery Ferments* and *Fermented Vegetables*

"Michael has an amazing ability to create beautifully delicious, spicy dishes while at the same time making them both inspiring and totally approachable for the everyday cook or the wild-eyed chilihead!"

—**Jeremy Walsh,** founder of Bigfat's Hot Sauce, Inc.

"*The Spicy Food Lovers' Cookbook* is a beautiful marriage of flavor and heat."

—**Isabel Orozco-Moore,** founder and photographer of Isabel Eats

THE
SPICY FOOD
LOVERS'
Cookbook

Fiery, No-Fuss Meals

MICHAEL HULTQUIST

author of *The Spicy Dehydrator Cookbook*

PAGE STREET
PUBLISHING CO.

Copyright © 2018 Michael J. Hultquist

First published in 2018 by

Page Street Publishing Co.

27 Congress Street, Suite 105

Salem, MA 01970

www.pagestreetpublishing.com

Distributed by Macmillan, sales in Canada by The Canadian Manda Group.

22   21   20   19   18   1   2   3   4   5

ISBN-13: 978-1-62414-639-8

ISBN-10: 1-62414-639-2

Library of Congress Control Number: 2018938280

Cover and book design by Laura Gallant for Page Street Publishing Co.

Photography by Patty Hultquist

Printed and bound in the United States

This book is dedicated to all the creative cooks in the world who have found a passion for food and feel the need to keep on learning and exploring.

It is dedicated to all the bold and spicy food lovers who visit our blog at Chili Pepper Madness—www.chilipeppermadness.com. We couldn't do what we do without your support. Truly, all of your comments and support mean so much to me.

And finally, to my wife, partner and best friend—Patty. You are amazing beyond compare. You inspire me, always.

Contents

INTRODUCTION

I grew up with a pretty boring palate. I remember as a kid wanting nothing but grilled cheese sandwiches and boiled hot dogs. My mother cooked, though she wasn't big on seasonings, and it was pretty much your typical Midwestern fare. The spiciest thing I ever ate as a kid was from the local Taco Bell—it was just what I was used to.

It wasn't until I went off to college that I began to discover foods with real flavor. One of my roommates was Mexican and when we made chili together, he would season the heck out of it. It was then that I discovered the burgeoning world of hot sauces and found myself hooked. Who knew there were more hot sauces out there than just your mass market stuff?

I quickly realized I was a total chilihead. I found that I loved spicy foods; the spicier the better. Soon, I was drawn to the wild world of artisan hot sauces and chili peppers. While at the market, I would snatch up hot sauces by the armload and bought peppers by the bagful.

I took to cooking not long after I married and found myself incorporating peppers and other spicy elements into just about everything I made. After a while, I decided to share this particular passion by starting a food blog called Chili Pepper Madness, where I still explore cooking with chili peppers of all types, as well as detail how to grow and preserve them.

On a patch by the side of our first home, my wife and I started a garden where I grew my very first jalapeño plant. Now, we have a good-sized pepper patch in our backyard, where I grow a couple dozen different types every year. I just can't get enough of them.

It isn't ONLY chili peppers for me, though. All of this passion arose from that very first desire for SPICINESS. More than anything, it was FLAVOR that I craved in my life. I was bored of the plain and the bland. I needed some oomph—some zest!

Imagine my delight when I found my very first authentic Mexican restaurant, my first Indian place, then Thai, Cajun, Chinese, Southern Barbecue. The list goes on. So many great cuisines in the world! So many wonderful, creative ways to encounter bold flavors!

I'm sure my excitement is obvious. It's the same way for you, though, isn't it? I'm not sure on what level you consider yourself a spicy foodie, but you've been bitten by that bug, haven't you? Maybe you're even a full on chilihead and you don't even know it. Maybe you're like me and you just can't deal with the boring and the bland. Life is too short for that, isn't it?

I hope this cookbook helps you find the fiery flavors you crave. These are some of my very favorite recipes, and as a collection, represent how I like to eat. The goal is to make them both easy and spicy.

Let's get cooking!

Michael J Hultquist

Please note that...

SPICY DOES NOT ALWAYS MEAN HOT

Some people think spicy food means blazing hot food, but that isn't always the case. Consider Cajun cuisine, which isn't hot in many cases, but is filled with amazing flavor. Spicy just means you're using a lot of different herbs and spices in your food. It isn't necessarily the amount of spices, but the types you're using, as well as the combination of spices.

But, don't get me wrong. I do LOVE my HEAT. Most of these recipes will deliver both spice AND heat, so be prepared. However, you can easily adjust to your own heat level preference.

You'll notice that I rely heavily on chili peppers to add both heat and spice to my recipes, though I also rely greatly on a good collection of spices and other condiments to make meals truly tasty. In the condiments section (page 180) of the book, you will find a list of some of the ingredients I use the most.

As a chili pepper enthusiast, I cook with many, many different types of chili peppers, though I mostly grow them. I realize many of them will not be readily accessible to most, so these recipes incorporate peppers of various heat ranges that you should be able to find in most grocery stores. You will find heavy usage here of bells and poblanos, jalapeños, serranos, cayennes, habaneros and a smattering of ghost peppers here and there. You should be able to find these locally, but if not, you are free to swap in peppers of similar heat ranges.

MY APPROACH TO THIS BOOK

My focus is on flavor first, with heat second. There is no reason for you to eat something that is too hot for you. At the end of each recipe, I discuss ways you can dial down the heat and spice factors to suit your tastes. I also offer tips on how to increase those factors, since there are people, like myself, who love their food with a good amount of heat.

I've rated the spice level of each recipe to indicate the overall heat level, considering a general spicy-food-loving audience. I used the following levels as a barometer:

MILD: Includes bell peppers, poblanos and certain dried Mexican varieties.

MEDIUM: About as hot as your typical jalapeño pepper or equivalent.

MEDIUM-HOT: About as hot as your typical serrano pepper or equivalent.

HOT: About as hot as your typical habanero pepper, Scotch bonnet or equivalent.

VERY HOT: Ghost pepper level heat and above.

Please bear in mind that many chili pepper varieties offer a range of heat levels, so one jalapeño might give you a hotter dish than another, but you can alter these recipes to include different peppers and spices to please your palate.

Other seasoning blends and ingredients can also affect the overall heat level, so I've taken those into account in my ratings as well.

My goal in writing this book is to help you make meals that are easy and don't require too many steps or ingredients. Many of the recipes can be made in 30 minutes or less, but some will require about an hour. The slow cooker recipes will need longer, but they're mostly just waiting, so you can set them and forget about them until you're ready to eat. If you don't have a pressure cooker or an Instant Pot, I highly encourage you to get one. You can enjoy meals that normally require long cooking in a fraction of the time.

TAMING THE HEAT

Sometimes when cooking with chili peppers and other spicy foods, you find that you've added a bit too much heat to your meal. It happens, but that doesn't mean the meal is ruined. There are ways to temper that overall heat and spice.

The following method will work only BEFORE you've started cooking. Most of the heat in chili peppers is concentrated in the whitish innards, so if you core them out before cooking, you'll reduce the overall heat. Just be sure to wear gloves. This isn't necessarily true, though, of very hot chili peppers like ghost peppers and above, as the capsaicin (the chemical that makes the peppers hot) stretches into the skins more deeply.

DAIRY: Dairy contains a chemical, casein, which attracts capsaicin molecules, stripping them away from your tongue. If you feel too much of a burn, drink milk or consume another dairy, such as sour cream or cottage cheese. You can also add some dairy to your meal, depending on what you've prepared.

SUGAR: In a pinch, a bit of sugar can help absorb chili pepper heat. Don't overdo it, though.

DILUTION: If you've made a big pot of spicy food—for example, a chili or gumbo—you can always add other ingredients to dilute the overall heat factor. You'll wind up with a much larger batch, but at least you can freeze the leftovers or refrigerate them for eating later in the week.

ABSORBING FOODS: If it fits the recipe, try serving the meal over plain rice or pasta, which can help dilute and absorb the heat. You can also use bread to soak things up.

From the Land
(of Intensity!)

You can easily satisfy your spicy-food-loving palate with dinner stars like pork tenderloin, a thick-cut steak or different cuts of chicken. Chicken is a type of protein that absorbs all those powerful flavors you throw at it and gives them right back to you in the most satisfying way.

Pork flavors vary from cut to cut, but it can handle big doses of spice. Red meat like steak or lamb are powerhouses in the kitchen, working to satisfy the heartiest of appetites.

Here I've included several chicken recipes, using different parts of the chicken, as well as a couple of pork dishes that I love. I've also chosen one of my favorite ways to prepare steak, and a recipe for lamb chops that is sure to land a spot on your list of favorites.

Let's spice it up!

PREP
TIME

10 minutes

COOKING
TIME

35 minutes

SERVES

4

HEAT
LEVEL

Hot

Spicy Smothered
CREOLE PORK CHOPS

These bone-in pork chops are generously seasoned, seared and then smothered in a thick, spicy gravy that coats every bite. I use Mexican crema to bring a creamy element to the recipe, but try heavy cream for a more decadent version.

2 tbsp (30 ml) olive oil, divided

4 thin-cut (about ¾" [2-cm]) bone-in pork chops

2–3 tbsp (30–45 g) Creole seasoning blend

1 tsp garlic powder

Salt and pepper to taste

1 small sweet onion, chopped

1 red bell pepper, chopped

1 habanero pepper, chopped

3 cloves garlic, chopped

2 tbsp (16 g) all-purpose flour

1 cup (240 ml) chicken stock

2 tbsp (30 g) Mexican crema or sour cream

Hot sauce, diced sweet peppers and fresh chopped parsley, for serving

Heat a large pan to medium heat and add a tablespoon (15 ml) of olive oil. Season the pork chops generously with the Creole seasoning, garlic powder, salt and plenty of cracked black pepper. Sear them in the hot pan for 5 minutes per side to get a nice brown color on them. Take them out of the pan and set them aside on a plate.

In the same pan, add a bit more olive oil and add the onion and peppers. Cook them down for a couple of minutes, until they begin to soften. Add the garlic cloves and cook for another minute, or until fragrant.

Stir in the flour and more Creole seasoning, if desired, and cook for another minute; then pour in the chicken stock. Stir it for a couple of minutes, until the mixture thickens up into a gravy. For a thinner sauce, add in a bit more stock.

Swirl in the crema, then nestle the pork chops back into the sauce. Simmer for another 15 to 20 minutes, or until the pork chops are cooked through. Garnish with hot sauce, sweet peppers and parsley.

TWEAK THE HEAT: You'll get some good heat with the habanero pepper. If you'd like to tame the heat, you can either core out the habanero innards, or omit the habanero altogether, though I love this level of heat. You can also easily adjust the amount of Creole seasoning used.

Sweet Chili–Glazed
BACON-WRAPPED PORK TENDERLOIN

Your favorite pepper jam makes for a quick and easy glaze when combined with a couple of other simple ingredients. No need to whip one together from scratch. The resulting tenderloin is tender, slightly sweet and big on flavor.

1–1½ lb (450–681 g) pork tenderloin
1–2 tbsp (12–24 g) Cajun seasoning blend
1 tbsp (9 g) garlic powder
Salt and pepper to taste
8 slices bacon

¾ cup (245 g) red pepper jam
2 tbsp (30 ml) red wine vinegar
2 tbsp (30 ml) of your favorite hot sauce
Side veggies of your choice, for serving

Preheat the oven to 400°F (200°C).

Pat the pork tenderloin dry and lay it flat on a cutting board. Season it liberally with the Cajun seasoning, garlic powder, salt and pepper.

Next, tuck the thinner end of the tenderloin underneath to keep an even thickness, then wrap it with bacon. Try to overlap the bacon, as the bacon will shrink a bit while cooking. Place the tenderloin inside a baking dish or ovenproof pan.

In a medium bowl, combine the pepper jam, red wine vinegar and hot sauce. Spoon about a third of the glaze over the bacon-wrapped tenderloin and gently massage it over the meat. A basting mop works great here.

Bake for 20 minutes, then mop the tenderloin with another third of the glaze.

Place it back in the oven and bake for 10 to 15 minutes for an internal temperature of 160°F (71°C) for medium-well.

Remove it from the oven and let it rest for 3 minutes. Spoon on the remaining glaze. Slice and serve with veggies of your choice, such as roasted carrots or mashed potatoes.

TWEAK THE HEAT: Your heat levels can vary widely based on your choices of pepper jam and hot sauce. Most pepper jams are pleasantly sweet with low levels of heat, if any at all, but hot sauces range wildly in heat. Choose one based on your tastes and heat preferences.

PREP TIME

10 minutes

COOKING TIME

30 minutes

SERVES

4

HEAT LEVEL

Mild-Hot (Depending on your choices of pepper jam and hot sauce)

PREP
TIME

15 minutes

COOKING
TIME

75 to 90
minutes

SERVES

6

HEAT
LEVEL

Medium-Hot

Three Pepper–Rubbed
ROASTED WHOLE CHICKEN

There is nothing complicated about roasting a whole chicken. It just takes a bit of time, though it is almost all cooking time. You'll make short work of the prep by whipping together an easy chili paste that will add big flavor to your bird. Rub it down and pop it in the oven. All you have to do is wait, then eat!

1 (5–6 lb [2.2–2.7 kg]) whole roasting chicken
2 habanero peppers, chopped
4 serrano peppers, chopped
2 jalapeño peppers, chopped, plus extra for roasting
3 cloves garlic
Juice from 1 lime
¾ cup (12 g) cilantro, chopped

¼ cup olive oil plus 1 tbsp (75 ml), divided
1 tbsp (6 g) cumin
Salt and pepper to taste
3 medium-sized potatoes
½ cup (120 ml) chicken broth or water
1 lemon, quartered
Side veggies of your choice, for serving

Preheat your oven to 400°F (200°C).

Wash and pat dry the chicken. Remove any giblets from the cavity.

In a medium bowl, add the peppers, garlic, lime juice, cilantro, ¼ cup (60 ml) olive oil, cumin and a pinch of salt and pepper. Process it to form a thick, spicy chili paste.

Use it to rub down the entire chicken. Lift the skin over the breast to get underneath, and add some inside the cavity. It will add a lot of flavor.

Peel and chop the potatoes and toss them with a tablespoon (15 ml) of olive oil and some salt and pepper. Set them into the bottom of a large baking dish. Pour the broth over the potatoes.

Quarter the lemon and stuff it into the cavity, and set the chicken on top of the potatoes.

Bake the chicken for 75 to 90 minutes, or until it reaches an internal temperature of 165°F (74°C) with a meat thermometer.

Remove from the heat and set on a serving platter for carving. Serve with veggies of your choice.

Peppercorn-Crusted
RIB EYE WITH CHILI CHIMICHURRI ROJO

No need to spend your hard-earned money at the local steak house when you can prepare them at home. Rib eyes are particularly easy to prepare as they cook up in minutes, and they're highly marbled so you are guaranteed a juicy, flavorful dinner. This is served with an easy-to-prepare sauce that is popular in South America.

PREP TIME

10 minutes

COOKING TIME

6 to 8 minutes

SERVES

2-4

HEAT LEVEL

Mild

FOR THE STEAKS

2 rib eye steaks (8 oz [227 g] each, ¾" [2-cm]-thick cut)

2 tbsp (17 g) black peppercorns (or just use coarsely ground black pepper)

1 tbsp (18 g) sea salt

1 tbsp (15 ml) olive oil

2 tbsp (29 g) butter

Fresh parsley, optional

Crushed garlic cloves, optional

FOR THE CHIMICHURRI ROJO

¼ cup (60 ml) olive oil

3 tbsp (45 ml) red wine vinegar

1 large red bell pepper (or use hotter peppers, if desired)

¼ cup (15 g) chopped parsley

¼ cup (4 g) chopped cilantro

3 cloves garlic, crushed

Salt and pepper to taste

Side veggies of your choice, for serving

First, pat the steaks dry with a paper towel. Coarsely crush up the peppercorns with a mortar and pestle, or use the coarse setting on your pepper grinder. Generously season each side of the steaks with the coarse pepper and sea salt. Use a fork to rub the seasonings into the meat.

In a large pan, heat the olive oil and sear the steaks for 3 minutes, then flip them. Next, melt the butter into the pan. For extra flavor, add in a spoonful of fresh parsley or even crushed garlic cloves. Use a spoon to baste the steaks in the butter.

Cook the steaks for 3 to 5 minutes, until they are done to your preference, while continuing to baste in the butter. Three minutes will give you a nice, medium-rare sear.

Remove the steaks from the pan and set them on serving plates to rest.

In a food processor, add the olive oil, red wine vinegar, red bell pepper, parsley, cilantro, garlic and salt and pepper to taste. Process until smooth. Spoon some of the chimichurri over the steaks and serve them up with your favorite veggies.

TWEAK THE HEAT: Chimichurri is not traditionally hot, though it is filled with big flavor from the combination of oil and herbs. You can very easily toss a hot pepper into the mix, anywhere from a jalapeño to a fiery Scotch bonnet, to up the heat level to your preference.

PREP
TIME

10 minutes

COOKING
TIME

40 minutes

SERVES

4

HEAT
LEVEL

Medium

Honey-Sriracha
BAKED CHICKEN LEGS

The combination of sweet honey, spicy sriracha and tart lime juice makes for a super quick sauce for chicken legs. Prep is a breeze—just a bit of chopping, whisking and seasoning. All you have to do is pop these into the oven and wait.

FOR THE CHICKEN
6–8 chicken legs

1 tbsp (7 g) smoked paprika

1 tsp cayenne powder

1 tsp garlic powder

1 tsp baking powder

Salt and pepper to taste

1 lime, sliced

1–2 jalapeño peppers, sliced

Fresh chopped cilantro, for serving

FOR THE POTATOES
¾ lb (340 g) small potatoes (I used yellow and purple), quartered

1 tbsp (15 ml) olive oil

1 tsp cayenne powder

1 tsp garlic powder

Salt and pepper to taste

FOR THE SAUCE
4 tbsp (60 ml) sriracha

4 tbsp (80 g) honey

1 tbsp (15 ml) lime juice

Preheat the oven to 450°F (230°C).

In a bowl, toss the chicken legs with the paprika, cayenne, garlic powder, baking powder, salt and pepper. Coat them well. The baking powder helps with the overall crispiness. Set them into a lightly oiled baking dish or pan.

In a separate bowl, toss the potatoes with the olive oil, cayenne, garlic powder, salt and pepper. Scatter them into the baking dish around the chicken.

In a medium bowl, combine the sriracha, honey and lime juice. Brush the sauce on the chicken legs. Top everything with the lime slices and jalapeño pepper slices.

Bake for 10 minutes, then reduce the heat to 350°F (180°C) and continue to bake for 30 minutes, or until the chicken legs are cooked through. They should register 165°F (74°C) internally.

Sprinkle with fresh cilantro before serving.

HOT TIP: You can speed up the recipe a bit by heating a cast iron or other oven-safe pan on the stovetop first, then browning the chicken legs and potatoes in the pan before baking.

TWEAK THE HEAT: Add a bit more spice factor by making extra honey-sriracha sauce and brushing more on the legs after baking.

Lamb Chops with
GARLIC-CHILI PAN SAUCE

I'm a sucker for lamb chops. When we go out for special meals, I seek them out on the menu. Luckily for us, they're incredibly easy to prepare at home. I get my lamb chops trimmed and Frenched from the butcher. It saves time and you can pick them up on your way home.

You won't get a lot of heat factor with this dish, but you WILL get huge flavor. The buttery pan sauce is warm and slightly tart, and it clings to every nook and cranny of the lamb. You might need to double up on this recipe—it's so good.

PREP TIME

10 minutes

COOKING TIME

10 minutes

SERVES

4

HEAT LEVEL

Mild

FOR THE LAMB CHOPS

8 lamb chops (½" [1.3 cm] thick, about 2 lb [908 g])

1 tbsp (5 g) red chili flakes, plus more for serving

Salt and pepper to taste

3 tbsp (45 ml) olive oil

1–2 small red chilies, sliced

8 cloves garlic, thickly sliced

2 sprigs fresh thyme

FOR THE SAUCE

3 tbsp (45 ml) white wine

2 tbsp (29 g) butter

Juice from 1 lemon

1 tbsp (5 g) red chili flakes

2 tbsp (8 g) fresh chopped parsley, plus more for garnish

Season the lamb chops with 1 tablespoon (5 g) of the chili flakes, salt and pepper.

Heat a large pan to medium-high heat. Add the olive oil and heat through. Add the lamb chops, chili peppers, garlic and fresh thyme. Cook the chops for 3 to 4 minutes per side for a medium cook. Remove the chops and cover them with foil to keep warm. You may need to cook them in batches.

Add the white wine to the pan to deglaze it, scraping up the browned bits with a wooden spoon. Add the butter, lemon juice, chili flakes and chopped parsley. Stir and cook for about a minute.

Pour the pan sauce over the lamb chops and serve them with extra chili flakes and fresh parsley.

TWEAK THE HEAT: If you'd like to bring some extra zest factor, add more fresh garlic or extra chili flakes. Garlic really elevates the flavor and zing.

PREP
TIME

10 minutes

COOKING
TIME

45 minutes

SERVES

4

HEAT
LEVEL

Medium

Chicken Tinga–Loaded
BAKED POTATOES

Chicken Tinga is a popular Mexican comfort food of shredded chicken that's been simmered in a chipotle-tomato sauce. It is usually served on tortillas as tacos or tostadas, though I enjoy spooning it over a big oven-baked potato for something completely different. I love the combination of flavors. Extra pan-toasted jalapeños for me, please! I used chicken thighs for this dish, though you can use chicken breast if you'd like.

FOR THE CHICKEN
4 medium-sized baking potatoes
2 tbsp (30 ml) olive oil
1 tbsp (9 g) garlic powder
1 tbsp (18 g) salt
1 tsp ground black pepper
1 lb (454 g) chicken thighs, sliced in half

FOR THE SAUCE
1 tbsp (15 ml) olive oil
1 small onion, chopped
2 jalapeño peppers, chopped

3 cloves garlic, chopped
1 (15-oz [425-g]) can tomato sauce
1 (7-oz [198-g]) can of chipotles in adobo sauce
1 tbsp (9 g) Mexican oregano
Salt and pepper to taste

FOR THE PAN-TOASTED JALAPEÑOS
1 tbsp (15 ml) olive oil
2 jalapeño peppers, sliced thin

Shredded pepper Jack cheese and fresh chopped cilantro, for serving

Preheat the oven to 400°F (200°C). Toss the potatoes with 2 tablespoons (30 ml) of olive oil, then rub them down with the garlic powder, salt and pepper. You can go heavy on the seasoning if you'd like. Bake the potatoes for 45 minutes, unwrapped, until soft. The skins should be fairly crispy.

While the potatoes are baking, set the chicken thighs in a large pan and cover with water. Bring to a quick boil, then reduce the heat and simmer until the chicken is cooked through, about 15 minutes. Remove the chicken and shred it with forks. Set it aside.

While the chicken is cooking, heat a pan to medium heat and add a tablespoon (15 ml) of olive oil. Add the onion and peppers and cook them down for about 5 minutes. Add the garlic and cook another minute, until fragrant. Add the tomato sauce, chipotles in adobo sauce, oregano and salt and pepper. Stir to break up the chipotles and simmer for 15 minutes. Add the chicken and simmer until the potatoes are ready.

When the potatoes are done, cut them down the middle, but not all the way through. Use a fork to open them up. Spoon the saucy chicken into the potatoes, then top with the shredded pepper Jack cheese and fresh cilantro.

For the pan-toasted jalapeños, heat a small pan to medium heat. Add the oil and sliced jalapeños. Cook for a couple minutes, until the jalapeños soften and slightly char. Serve them over the potatoes.

HOT TIP: This recipe takes a bit longer because of the baking time for the potatoes, though it's still very easy to make. You can speed up the process by using your microwave to cook the potatoes.

Cheese and Jalapeño
STUFFED CHICKEN

If you enjoy jalapeño poppers, you'll enjoy this stuffed chicken that takes some of the most popular jalapeño popper ingredients and stuffs them into a chicken breast. The result is a spicy, cheesy combo in every bite. Works for me!

PREP TIME

10 minutes

COOKING TIME

30 minutes

SERVES

4

HEAT LEVEL

Medium-Hot

6 oz (170 g) cream cheese, softened

2 oz (57 g) shredded cheddar cheese

2 large jalapeño peppers, diced, plus more as desired

2 tbsp (30 ml) of your favorite hot sauce

2 tbsp (14 g) smoked paprika, divided

2 tbsp (18 g) garlic powder, divided

Salt and pepper to taste

4 medium-sized chicken breasts

2 tbsp (30 ml) olive oil

Cherry tomatoes (optional)

Fresh chopped cilantro and your choice of veggies, for serving

In a medium bowl, create the stuffing mixture by combining the cream cheese, cheddar cheese, jalapeño peppers, hot sauce, a tablespoon (7 g) of paprika, a tablespoon (9 g) of garlic powder and a pinch of salt and pepper. Mix well.

Next, slice a pocket into each chicken with a small knife. Cut about three-quarters of the way into each chicken breast from the side, careful not to cut all the way through. Spoon the cheese mixture into each pocket and secure the openings with toothpicks.

Season the chicken breasts with the remaining tablespoon (7 g) of paprika and tablespoon (9 g) garlic powder, plus a bit of salt and pepper.

Heat a large pan to medium heat and add the olive oil. Sear each chicken breast for about 5 minutes, then flip to the other side, being careful not to spill out the cheese stuffing. At this point, I like to toss in some extra jalapeño slices and a few cherry tomatoes.

Cook for another 5 minutes to get a good sear, then cover the chicken and reduce the heat. Cook for 15 to 20 minutes, or until the chicken is cooked through completely. It should register 165°F (74°C) internally. Sprinkle on some fresh cilantro and serve with your favorite veggie side.

TWEAK THE HEAT: You'll get a fairly good spicy heat level from the jalapeño peppers, though they aren't overly spicy. If you're looking for higher heat, you can add in a hotter pepper (e.g., cayenne, serrano or habanero peppers). You can also add in more of your favorite hot sauce, as well as a spicier alternative to smoked paprika, such as cayenne powder, or a nice artisan blend.

Sizzling Seafood

Seafood is always a quick and tasty option for easy meals. Shrimp and most fish cook in a fraction of the time of some other proteins, and they take to spicy additions like no other. Whenever I visit the coast, I make a point to get the freshest seafood available. It's so much better when you prepare it yourself.

I would be hard pressed to choose a favorite type of seafood. I love it all, from any type of white fish (and there is a HUGE variety) to shrimp, clams, crab, lobster, octopus—you name it. I do love my seafood.

I've included a collection of some of my favorites that are quick and easy to prepare, focusing on flavors that will grab hold of your taste buds and take them for a ride.

PREP
TIME

10 minutes

COOKING
TIME

20 to 30
minutes

SERVES

4

HEAT
LEVEL

Hot

Shrimp in Fiery
CHIPOTLE-TEQUILA SAUCE

This sauce is tangy and deeply flavored from the combination of chipotle sauce and tequila, but also fiery from the addition of serrano peppers, with a buttery finish. Serve it with crusty bread to sop up the extra sauce. If you can't find chipotle sauce, substitute a can of chipotles in adobo sauce that has been processed in a food processor. Beware. It is quite addictive.

FOR THE SAUCE
1 tbsp (15 ml) olive oil
3 serrano peppers, chopped
4 cloves garlic, chopped
1 stick butter (use only half a stick for a less buttery sauce)
2 (7-oz [198-g]) cans chipotle sauce
3 oz (90 ml) white tequila
4 tbsp (80 g) honey

FOR THE SHRIMP
1½ lbs (681 g) shrimp, peeled and deveined

White rice, crusty bread and lime slices, for serving

In a large pan, heat the oil to medium heat. Add the serrano peppers and cook for a couple of minutes to soften them up. Add in the garlic and give it a quick stir. Cook for about a minute, or until fragrant.

Add the butter and swirl it until it melts, then stir in the chipotle sauce, tequila and honey. Reduce the heat and let it simmer for about 10 to 15 minutes to allow the flavors to meld a bit.

Add the shrimp and stir, making sure all the shrimp are covered with the sauce. Simmer for 10 to 15 minutes, or until the shrimp are cooked through, yet firm.

Serve in bowls over white rice and a side of crusty bread. Squeeze a bit of lime juice over each dish for a fresh pop of citrus.

HOT TIP: Instead of rice, try serving the shrimp on tortillas with avocado slices and fresh roasted chilies.

TWEAK THE HEAT: If you'd like to tame the heat, halve the amount of serrano peppers or substitute them with jalapeño peppers. For a bit more heat, add in your favorite hot peppers, such as habanero or even ghost pepper, for a truly fired-up recipe.

Spicy Ahi Tuna
POKE BOWLS

"Poke" is a Hawaiian dish of raw fish, which literally translates to "to slice." It is traditionally served with octopus or raw tuna, though I prefer to give the tuna a quick sear before tossing it with dressing. This adaptation adds some zing in the form of sriracha and thinly sliced hot peppers. It's super easy to prepare. Most of the work is in chopping veggies.

PREP TIME

20 minutes

COOKING TIME

15 minutes

SERVES

4

HEAT LEVEL

Medium

2 cups (322 g) cooked white rice

1 medium carrot, thinly chopped

1 cup (151 g) snow peas

1 large avocado, thinly sliced

1 small cucumber, thinly sliced

1 mango, cubed

2–3 hot peppers, thinly sliced

2 (6-oz [170-g]) tuna steaks

Salt and pepper to taste

1 tbsp (10 g) sesame seeds, plus more for garnish

1 tbsp (15 ml) olive oil

4 tbsp (60 ml) soy sauce, plus more for serving

2 tbsp (30 ml) sesame oil

1 tbsp (15 ml) sriracha

Hot pepper flakes, for serving

Cook the rice according to the package instructions, which should take less than 15 minutes. While the rice is cooking, chop the carrot, snow peas, avocado, cucumber, mango and hot peppers.

Next, season the tuna steaks with salt, pepper and sesame seeds. In a pan, heat the olive oil to medium heat and sear the tuna steaks for 30 to 45 seconds per side. You don't want to cook them all the way through. Remove them from the pan, let them cool slightly, then slice them into cubes roughly the same size as the cubed mango.

In a large bowl, combine the soy sauce, sesame oil and sriracha. Add the cubed tuna and toss to coat.

To make the bowls, add the rice to the bottom of the bowl, arrange the vegetables around the outer edge and place the seasoned tuna in the center.

Sprinkle with hot pepper flakes and extra sesame seeds. Serve with extra soy sauce. Don't forget the chopsticks!

HOT TIP: Consider making a version of this dish with salmon as well.

TWEAK THE HEAT: To tame the heat, use milder peppers and omit the hot pepper flakes. For a bit more spicy heat, add a bit of your favorite hot sauce.

PREP
TIME

10 minutes

COOKING
TIME

15 minutes

SERVES

4

HEAT
LEVEL

Mild-Medium

Tortilla–Crusted Swordfish
WITH SALSA CRIOLLA

Crushed corn tortillas add a distinctive flavor over your typical breadcrumbs and pair perfectly with an Argentinian salsa made with finely chopped peppers and other veggies. It isn't big in the heat department, but you'll love the vibrant flavor. Use a blender to achieve finely crushed tortillas.

FOR THE FISH
1 egg
1 cup (34 g) finely crushed corn tortilla chips
1 tbsp (7 g) cayenne powder
1 tsp smoked paprika
1 tsp garlic powder
1 tsp onion powder
Salt and pepper to taste
4 (5-oz [142-g]) swordfish steaks

Fresh chopped cilantro and lime wedges, for serving

FOR THE SALSA CRIOLLA
1 small red bell pepper, finely chopped
1 jalapeño pepper, finely chopped
½ small white onion, finely chopped
1 small tomato, chopped
1 clove garlic, minced
¼ cup (60 ml) olive oil
3 tbsp (45 ml) red wine vinegar
1 tsp crushed red pepper
1 tsp minced fresh oregano
Salt and pepper to taste

For the swordfish, heat the oven to 400°F (200°C).

In a wide bowl, beat the egg. In a separate bowl, combine the crushed tortilla chips, cayenne, paprika, garlic powder, onion powder, salt and pepper.

Pat the swordfish steaks dry and dip them into the egg. Be sure to get each side. Toss them in the seasoned tortilla crumb mixture. Make sure each side is evenly coated.

Set the steaks onto a lightly oiled baking sheet and bake for 15 minutes, or until the steaks are nice and flaky.

In a large bowl, add the red bell pepper, jalapeño pepper, onion, tomato and garlic. In a separate bowl, combine the olive oil and vinegar. Pour it into the first bowl and toss to coat everything. Add the crushed red pepper, oregano, salt and pepper to your preference.

Give it a good stir and serve it with the swordfish steaks. Garnish with cilantro and lime wedges.

TWEAK THE HEAT: You can easily elevate the heat and spice factor by increasing the amount of seasonings used, particularly the chili flakes and cayenne powder. You can also introduce spicier peppers.

Southern Shrimp and Grits

My wife and I fell in love with shrimp and grits while visiting Florida, and we've made it our mission to try as many versions as we can every time we travel to the South. Creamy, cheesy grits topped with a savory tomato sauce and filled with smoky andouille and succulent shrimp make for extraordinary flavors and textures. Some versions can take hours to prepare, but I have perfected this simple version which, in my opinion, stands up to them all.

PREP TIME

15 minutes

COOKING TIME

20 minutes

SERVES

4

HEAT LEVEL

Medium–Hot

FOR THE SHRIMP

1 tbsp (15 ml) olive oil

1 red bell pepper, diced

1 jalapeño pepper, diced

1 small sweet onion, diced

1 stalk celery, diced

3 cloves garlic, chopped

2 tbsp (16 g) all-purpose flour

2 tbsp (24 g) Cajun seasoning blend

1 tsp cayenne powder

1 (6-oz [170-g]) andouille sausage, chopped

1½ cups (360 ml) chicken broth

1 (15-oz [425-g]) can fire roasted tomatoes

¼ cup (60 g) Mexican crema or sour cream

1 lb (454 g) shrimp, peeled and deveined

FOR THE GRITS

½ cup (85 g) quick grits

3 cups (720 ml) chicken broth

1 cup (130 g) shredded pepper Jack cheese (or more if desired)

½ cup (120 g) Mexican crema or sour cream

Salt and pepper to taste

Fresh parsley, for garnish

Heat a large pan to medium heat and add the olive oil. Add the bell pepper, jalapeño pepper, onion and celery and cook for 6 to 7 minutes, or until soft. Add the garlic and cook for another minute.

Stir in the flour, Cajun seasoning, cayenne and andouille sausage. Cook for a minute or so, while stirring.

Pour in the chicken broth and fire roasted tomatoes. Bring to a quick boil, then reduce the heat and simmer for 10 minutes. Swirl in the crema or sour cream until the sauce is slightly creamy.

Add the shrimp and cook for 2 to 3 minutes, or until the shrimp are cooked through and have achieved a pink color.

While the sauce is simmering, add the grits and chicken broth to a pot and bring to a quick boil. Reduce the heat and simmer for 5 to 7 minutes, until creamy.

Remove from the heat and stir in the pepper Jack cheese and crema, until melted. Adjust for salt and pepper.

Spoon the grits into bowls, then top with scoops of the tomato sauce with shrimp and chopped sausage. Garnish with fresh parsley.

TWEAK THE HEAT: You can reduce the heat by removing the cayenne and limiting the Cajun seasonings. For a spicier version, be generous with the Cajun seasonings and cayenne. You can even substitute spicier peppers for the jalapeño peppers.

PREP
TIME

15 minutes

COOKING
TIME

20 minutes

MAKES

6 crab cakes

HEAT
LEVEL

Mild–Medium

Easy Crab Cakes with
SPICY RÉMOULADE

Good crab cakes are light, delicate and easier to prepare than you might think. Just mix the ingredients together in a bowl, form the patties and cook them in a pan. This recipe uses Old Bay Seasoning from Maryland, where people dash it over everything, particularly steamed blue crab.

My wife and I visited the Chesapeake Bay in Maryland and caught 1 bushel of blue crab. I had a cook at a restaurant steam them for us so we could drive them back home in a cooler. He asked me if I wanted them seasoned, and of course I said yes. He asked me, "Do you want them mild? Or regular?" Apparently, spicy is "regular" up in the Chesapeake Bay area. Long story short, he steamed them up nice and spicy for us.

FOR THE CRAB CAKES
¾ cup (44 g) bread crumbs or crushed saltine crackers
2 tbsp (14 g) Old Bay Seasoning (or more to taste)
1 tsp garlic powder
Salt and pepper to taste
1 egg, beaten
2 tbsp (28 g) mayonnaise
1 tbsp (15 ml) of your favorite hot sauce
1 tbsp (16 g) whole-grain spicy mustard
1 tsp Worcestershire sauce
Juice from 1 lemon
1 tbsp (4 g) fresh chopped parsley

1 lb (454 g) fresh lump crab meat
2 tbsp (30 ml) olive oil

FOR THE RÉMOULADE
½ cup (112 g) mayonnaise
1 tbsp (16 g) whole-grain spicy mustard
2 tbsp (30 g) prepared horseradish
1 tbsp (15 ml) of your favorite hot sauce
1 tsp apple cider vinegar
1 tsp Old Bay Seasoning
Juice from ½ lemon
2 cloves garlic, minced

Lemon wedges or lettuce leaves, for serving

In a large bowl, combine the bread crumbs, Old Bay Seasoning, garlic powder, salt and pepper to make the crab cakes. Mix well.

In a separate bowl, combine the egg, mayonnaise, hot sauce, mustard, Worcestershire sauce, lemon juice and parsley.

Pour the wet ingredients into the dry and mix with a fork. Add the crab meat and hand mix. Form them into 6 crab cakes and set them on a large plate.

Next, make the rémoulade by processing the mayonnaise, mustard, horseradish, hot sauce, apple cider vinegar, Old Bay Seasoning, lemon juice and minced garlic in a food processor until smooth. Pour into a bowl and refrigerate until ready to use.

Heat a large pan to medium heat and add the olive oil. Add the crab cakes and cook them for 3 to 4 minutes per side, or until they are nicely browned on both sides. Serve with the spicy rémoulade and lemon wedges. Alternatively, serve them over lettuce leaves.

Jamaican-Spiced Salmon
WITH COCONUT-MANGO RICE

Jamaican jerk seasoning is an aromatic, highly flavorful blend of spices that adds a distinctive zest to any dish, particularly seafood. I make a blend at home that includes allspice, cinnamon, thyme, nutmeg, clove, onion powder, garlic powder, parsley, cayenne, paprika, chili flakes, cumin, sugar, salt and pepper. That's a lot of spice! It isn't hot, but it's BIG on flavor. Grab yourself a good blend from your grocer or online for recipes like this.

PREP TIME

10 minutes

COOKING TIME

15 minutes

SERVES

4

HEAT LEVEL

Medium-Hot

FOR THE SALMON
4 (6-oz [170-g]) salmon fillets

3 tbsp (21 g) Jamaican jerk seasoning

1 tbsp (8 g) all-purpose flour

2 tbsp (28 g) coconut oil

1 Scotch bonnet chili pepper, sliced

1 medium-sized sweet pepper (e.g. banana pepper), sliced, if desired

2 tbsp (29 g) butter

1 tbsp (20 g) honey

FOR THE RICE
1 cup (211 g) rice

2 cups (475 ml) water or chicken broth

2 tbsp (28 g) coconut oil

1 tbsp (18 g) salt, plus more as needed

1 mango, peeled and chopped

¼ cup (7 g) chopped basil, plus more for garnish

Limes and chopped peppers, for serving

Rub the salmon down with the Jamaican jerk seasoning and flour. Make sure they are evenly coated. Set them aside.

In a pot, add the rice, water, coconut oil and salt. Bring to a quick boil, then reduce the heat and simmer for about 15 minutes, or until the rice has absorbed the liquid and becomes fluffy.

While the rice is simmering, add 2 tablespoons (28 g) of the coconut oil to a large pan and bring to medium heat. Add the salmon and cook for about 5 minutes per side, or until they are mostly cooked through.

In a large pan, add the Scotch bonnet pepper, your choice of sweet pepper and butter. Allow the butter to melt. Drizzle in the honey and swirl the pan around to let the honey and butter combine. Spoon baste the salmon with the sweetened butter mixture, about a minute or so. Make sure to cover every nook and cranny.

Mix the mango and basil into the rice and salt to taste. Serve the rice on plates, then top it with salmon. Garnish with fresh chopped basil, fresh lime and chopped peppers, if desired.

TWEAK THE HEAT: If you can't find Scotch bonnets, habaneros are a very good substitute. You can limit the heat by either coring out the peppers first, or by using only half the Scotch bonnet. You can also go with a milder pepper, though you might lose the distinctive fruitiness of the Scotch bonnet. Add 2 or 3 peppers for extra heat.

PREP
TIME

10 minutes

COOKING
TIME

15 minutes

SERVES

4

HEAT
LEVEL

Medium

Shrimp Fajita Bowls with
CILANTRO-LIME RICE

Fajita bowls are always a dinner win. There is practically no prep work outside of chopping the vegetables, and everything cooks up fast in a big skillet. You can easily serve these over warmed flour tortillas with your favorite fixings, though I like to serve it over flavored rice. Try this with sliced chicken as well.

FOR THE SHRIMP

1½ lbs (681 g) shrimp, peeled and deveined

4 tbsp (60 ml) olive oil, divided

3 tbsp (9 g) fajita seasoning (homemade or store-bought)

2 medium-sized bell peppers, stemmed and sliced

4 jalapeño peppers, stemmed and sliced

1 medium white onion, sliced

1 cup (149 g) cherry tomatoes, sliced

¼ cup (60 ml) water

1 sliced avocado, fresh sliced limes and spicy chili flakes, for serving

FOR THE RICE

1 cup (211 g) long jasmine rice

1½ cups (360 ml) water

1 tbsp (18 g) salt

2 tbsp (2 g) chopped cilantro, plus more for serving

1 tsp cumin

Juice from 1 lime

In a large bowl, add the shrimp, 2 tablespoons (30 ml) of the olive oil and fajita seasoning blend. Toss to coat the shrimp evenly. Refrigerate until needed.

Add the rice, 1½ cups (360 ml) of water and salt and cook according to the package instructions, about 15 minutes or so, until fluffy. Stir in the cilantro, cumin and lime juice.

While the rice is cooking, make the pepper mixture. In a large saucepan, add 2 tablespoons (30 ml) of the olive oil, bell peppers, jalapeño peppers and onion. Cook them down for about 5 minutes, until they slightly soften. Stir in the shrimp and cook for 5 minutes or so, until the shrimp are cooked through. They should be a nice pink in the middle.

Add the cherry tomatoes with a ¼ cup (60 ml) of water and cook for a minute, until the water reduces and the sauce thickens.

Serve the rice in 4 bowls, then top with the shrimp-pepper mixture.

Top with the sliced avocado, fresh limes, fresh chopped cilantro and spicy chili flakes.

MIKE'S HOMEMADE FAJITA SEASONING BLEND

1 tsp cayenne powder

1 tsp paprika

1 tsp garlic powder

1 tsp onion powder

1 tsp dried oregano

1 tsp salt

½ tsp brown sugar

½ tsp cumin

¼ tsp ground black pepper

Spiced Tuna Steaks with
PINEAPPLE-JALAPEÑO SALSA

This recipe is a bit of a mash-up of different flavors, but it all comes together in one spicy dish. Tuna is great to cook with, as it only needs a few minutes to cook and is rich in flavor. If you're REALLY in a hurry, you can skip the marinating step, though I find the 30-minute wait is worth it.

PREP TIME

30 minutes

COOKING TIME

10 minutes

SERVES

4

HEAT LEVEL

Medium

FOR THE TUNA
¼ cup (60 ml) soy sauce
3 tbsp (45 ml) rice vinegar
3 tbsp (45 ml) chili oil, divided
1 tbsp (7 g) cayenne powder
1 tsp garlic powder
1 tsp dried ginger
Salt and pepper to taste
4 (6-oz [170-g]) tuna steaks

FOR THE SALSA
1 jalapeño pepper, chopped
1 cup (165 g) pineapple, chopped
1 small Roma tomato, chopped
1 tsp lime juice
3 tbsp (3 g) fresh cilantro, chopped

Your favorite veggies, for serving

In a medium bowl, combine the soy sauce, vinegar, 2 tablespoons (30 ml) of chili oil, cayenne, garlic, ginger and a pinch of salt and pepper. In a plastic bag or wide dish, pour the marinade over the tuna steaks. Cover and marinate in the refrigerator for 30 minutes.

While the tuna is marinating, make the salsa. In a small bowl, mix the jalapeño pepper, pineapple, tomato, lime juice and cilantro. Refrigerate until you're ready to use it.

In a large pan set to medium-high heat, add a tablespoon (15 ml) of the chili oil. Add the tuna steaks and sear for 2 to 3 minutes per side for medium-rare, or to your preference. Let the tuna rest for a couple of minutes.

Top with the pineapple-jalapeño salsa. Serve with your favorite veggies.

HOT TIP: I served ours with some asparagus that I tossed with chili oil and sautéed for a few minutes to soften, then finished them with a bit of sambal oelek for extra heat and flavor. Asparagus is great because it cooks up so quickly.

TWEAK THE HEAT: Your heat levels can vary for this recipe depending on the chili oil you've chosen. I often make my own chili oil at home from peppers I have grown in our garden, though you can usually find it at your grocer. If you have a hard time finding it, use olive oil instead with extra peppers or spicy chili flakes.

PREP
TIME

10 minutes

COOKING
TIME

15 minutes

SERVES

4

HEAT
LEVEL

Medium-Hot

Sheet Pan Thai-Glazed
RED SNAPPER WITH PEPPERS

Red snapper is a mild, flaky fish with a slightly sweet taste that lends itself perfectly to the heat of a good Thai glaze. If you're unable to find snapper, look for other white fish with a fairly firm texture, such as mahi-mahi, halibut or grouper. You can also make this with salmon, and though the flavor is completely different, it's definitely delicious.

4 (6-oz [170-g]) red snapper fillets

1 tbsp (7 g) hot paprika

1 tbsp (9 g) garlic powder

Salt and pepper to taste

Olive oil or spray oil, as needed

1 red bell pepper, sliced

1 green bell pepper, sliced

1 yellow bell pepper, sliced

1 lime, sliced, plus juice from 1 lime

½ cup (120 ml) Thai chili sauce

¼ cup (60 ml) soy sauce

1 tbsp (15 ml) sesame oil

1 tsp fresh grated ginger

1 tsp red pepper flakes, plus more for serving

Chopped fresh parsley and sesame seeds, for serving

Preheat the oven to 400°F (200°C).

Season the snapper with the hot paprika, garlic powder, salt and pepper. Set the fillets on a lightly oiled baking sheet. Surround the fillets with the chopped red, green and yellow bell peppers. Top with the lime slices.

Combine the Thai chili sauce, soy sauce, sesame oil, ginger, lime juice and red pepper flakes. Use half of the sauce to baste the fish and lightly baste the peppers.

Cover with foil and bake for 10 minutes. Remove the foil and return to the oven. Set the oven to broil and cook for 5 minutes, until the fish is cooked through and the vegetables are softened.

Remove from the oven and brush the fillets and peppers with the remaining glaze, then squeeze a bit of lime juice over everything. Garnish with red pepper flakes, chopped parsley and sesame seeds.

TWEAK THE HEAT: You'll get quite a bit of zing factor with this Thai chili glaze and the red pepper flakes, though if you're looking to up the heat factor, go heavy on the glaze and pepper flakes. You can also incorporate spicier peppers into the bell pepper mix, depending on your preference. If you're looking for a milder version, skip the chili flakes and go easy on the Thai chili sauce.

Hot & Spicy Handhelds

When it comes to easy dinners, it doesn't get much easier than piling something onto a few tortillas or between a couple buns. Quick and easy, though, doesn't have to mean boring and bland. Nor does it need to equate to your typical fast food fare. No way!

These handhelds are just right for dinner, won't stress you out in the kitchen and will leave your bellies filled and satisfied.

We're talking easy-to-make burgers that bring the heat, tacos that tingle the tongue and sandwiches that truly sizzle. While not every recipe here is meant to focus on being "hot," you can easily adjust to your preferred heat levels. Each dish delivers hugely when it comes to flavor and spice.

PREP
TIME

15 minutes

COOKING
TIME

10 minutes

MAKES

4 (¼-lb
[113-g]) smash
burgers, or
2 large
double-
deckers for a
big appetite

HEAT
LEVEL

Hot

Habanero Popper and
GUACAMOLE SMASH BURGERS

There aren't many foods more satisfying than a juicy smash burger, and they're simple to prepare. With a smash burger, it's all about the ground beef. Choose the best quality of 80/20 beef you can find. All you need for seasoning is salt and pepper, and whatever toppings you're in the mood for. Here is a spicy habanero popper version with creamy guacamole.

FOR THE GUACAMOLE
1 large avocado, pitted and peeled
2 tbsp (2 g) cilantro, chopped
Juice from ½ small lime
Pinch of salt

FOR THE CREAM CHEESE-PEPPER MIXTURE
6 oz (170 g) cream cheese, softened
2 tbsp (30 ml) sriracha
1 tsp garlic powder
Pinch of salt

1 tbsp (15 ml) olive oil
3 habanero peppers, sliced

FOR THE BURGERS
1 tbsp (15 ml) olive oil
1 lb (454 g) 80/20 ground beef
Salt and pepper to taste
Buns, for serving

In a small bowl, smash the avocado, cilantro, lime juice and a few grinds of salt to make the guacamole. Mix well. Taste and adjust for salt. Refrigerate until needed.

In a separate small bowl, combine the cream cheese, sriracha, garlic powder and a pinch of salt. Set it aside for now.

In a pan, heat a tablespoon (15 ml) of the oil and add the habanero pepper slices. Cook them for about 5 minutes to give them a light char. Remove them from the heat and set aside. In the same pan, heat a tablespoon (15 ml) olive oil.

Divide the beef into 4 pieces and form balls. Set them in the pan one at a time and smash them down with a spatula. You can also do this on a grill with proper grates. Season the burgers with salt and pepper.

Cook for a couple of minutes, until the bottoms begin to crisp up.

Flip and press with the spatula. Season with more salt and pepper and cook for a couple more minutes, until each side is crispy and done to about medium, or to your preference.

Serve the burgers in buns. Top with the cream cheese mixture, guacamole and habanero peppers.

TWEAK THE HEAT: Habaneros bring a high level of heat, so be prepared. Core them out if you'd like to tame the heat a bit.

Szechuan Salmon Tacos with
SERRANO-CUCUMBER SLAW

I love fish of all kinds, but if forced to choose a favorite, I'd probably go with salmon. It has the perfect amount of fat content and a meaty, yet flaky texture; plus, it can stand up to any number of cooking methods. When I saw salmon tacos on a menu at a quirky place in North Carolina, I knew I had to make my own version. This is my absolute favorite.

PREP TIME

15 minutes

COOKING TIME

10 minutes

MAKES

6 tacos

HEAT LEVEL

Medium-Hot

FOR THE SALMON
12 oz (340 g) salmon
¼ cup (60 ml) soy sauce
1 tbsp (7 g) cayenne powder
3 tbsp (45 ml) chili oil, divided
1 tbsp (9 g) garlic powder
Salt and pepper to taste
¾ cup (180 ml) Szechuan sauce
6 flour tortillas, warmed

FOR THE SLAW
1 small carrot, peeled and cut into rings
1 small cucumber, cut into rings
2–3 serrano peppers, cut into rings
2 tbsp (2 g) cilantro, chopped
2 tbsp (40 g) honey
3 tbsp (45 ml) white wine vinegar
Juice from ½ lime
Pinch of salt

Slice the salmon into 2-ounce (57-g) pieces and set them into a plastic bag. Pour in the soy sauce, cayenne, 2 tablespoons (30 ml) of chili oil, garlic powder and some salt and pepper.

Marinate for about 20 minutes while you make the crunchy slaw.

In a small bowl, slice the carrot and cucumber rings into very thin sticks. Add the serrano peppers and the cilantro.

In a separate bowl, whisk the honey, vinegar and lime juice. Then, pour it over the slaw. Give it a pinch of salt and toss it with a fork. Set the slaw aside until needed.

Next, heat the remaining tablespoon (15 ml) of chili oil in a large pan and add the salmon. Cook about 2 to 3 minutes per side, or until the salmon is cooked through. Add the Szechuan sauce and swirl to warm the sauce. Remove from heat.

Fill the tortillas with salmon and top with the spicy, crunchy slaw. Drizzle on extra Szechuan sauce, if you'd like.

TWEAK THE HEAT: Szechuan sauce is a sweet and spicy Asian cooking sauce that you can typically find in most grocery stores. There are many brands and each will have its own level of heat. If you find yours isn't as spicy as you'd like, add in a bit more cayenne powder to your marinade, or sprinkle a bit over the finished tacos. The serranos will provide a good level of heat for you, too.

PREP
TIME

10 minutes

COOKING
TIME

15 minutes

MAKES

4 turkey
burgers

HEAT
LEVEL

Mild (but
ZINGY!)

Turkey Burgers with
HORSERADISH CREAM
AND PICKLED PEPPERS

Turkey burgers often get a bad rap because they can be dry if they aren't properly prepared, and most restaurants don't give them the attention they deserve. Turkey has a much lower fat content than beef, but that is a strength, not a weakness. Since turkey is so much milder, it will reflect all those other ingredients you decide to include in your recipe. And, like this one, they can be quite juicy.

FOR THE BURGERS

1 medium red onion, minced

2 jalapeño peppers, minced

3 tsp (15 ml) olive oil, divided

3 cloves garlic, minced

1½ lbs (681 g) ground turkey

1 tbsp (7 g) cayenne powder

1 tsp smoked paprika

3 tbsp (48 g) spicy brown mustard

¼ cup (15 g) bread crumbs

Salt and pepper to taste

FOR THE HORSERADISH
CREAM SAUCE

4 tbsp (60 g) prepared horseradish

3 tbsp (45 g) sour cream or Mexican crema

2 tbsp (32 g) spicy brown mustard

1 tsp white wine vinegar

Pinch of salt

Buns, lettuce, sliced red onion and jarred pickled peppers, for serving

Heat a large pan to medium heat; add the onion, peppers and a teaspoon of olive oil. Cook for about 5 minutes to soften them up. Add the garlic and cook another minute, until fragrant.

Add the onion, peppers and garlic to a mixing bowl and let it cool slightly. Then, add the turkey, cayenne, paprika, mustard, 2 teaspoons (10 ml) of olive oil, bread crumbs, salt and pepper. Hand mix the meat mixture, but don't overmix or the turkey burgers will become mealy. Form into 4 burger patties.

Set the burgers into the still heated pan and cook for 5 minutes, then flip and sear the other side, about 3 minutes. Reduce the heat to low and cover with a lid; continue to cook for about 8 to 10 minutes, or until the turkey burgers are cooked through.

In a small bowl, whisk together the horseradish, sour cream, spicy brown mustard, vinegar and a pinch of salt.

Serve the burgers on the buns and drizzle with horseradish cream. Stack with lettuce, onion and loads of sweet pickled peppers.

TWEAK THE HEAT: These burgers don't have a lot of heat, but they get a lot of flavor and zing from the horseradish. You can easily change the ratio of horseradish to sour cream if you prefer more or less of that zing.

Mahi Mahi Tacos with
SESAME-GINGER SAUCE

When we hang in Florida, we visit a little restaurant/bar across the bridge that serves the best mahi mahi tacos I've ever tasted. They are by no means "fiery" to the tongue, but huge in the flavor department, so much so that I've been making my own version ever since. You will notice a bit of heat from the jalapeño slices and hot pepper flakes, but this recipe is more about the spicy flavor of the sesame-ginger sauce and how it mingles with the mild mahi mahi.

FOR THE MAHI MAHI
2 (6-oz [170-g]) mahi mahi fillets
1 tbsp (9 g) garlic powder
Salt and pepper to taste
1 tbsp (15 ml) olive oil

FOR THE SESAME-GINGER SAUCE
2 tbsp (30 ml) soy sauce
2 tbsp (30 ml) rice wine vinegar
1 tbsp (15 ml) sesame oil
1 clove garlic, minced
1 tsp minced fresh ginger
1 tsp hot pepper flakes, plus more for serving
1 tsp sugar

6 warmed flour tortillas, 2 cups (200 g) finely chopped red cabbage, 2 jalapeño peppers, 1 large tomato, diced, and hot sauce, for serving

PREP TIME	10 minutes
COOKING TIME	5 minutes
MAKES	6 tacos
HEAT LEVEL	Mild–Medium

Slice the mahi mahi into 2-ounce (57-g) pieces and set them into a bowl. Sprinkle them with garlic powder, salt and pepper.

In a small bowl, make the sauce by whisking together the soy sauce, rice wine vinegar, sesame oil, garlic, ginger, hot pepper flakes and sugar in a small bowl. Pour about half of it over the mahi mahi fillets and toss them until evenly coated.

Heat a pan to medium heat and add the olive oil. Cook the mahi mahi fillets for about 2 to 3 minutes per side, until they are cooked through.

Set each piece over warmed flour tortillas and spoon over a bit more of the sesame-ginger sauce. Top them with red cabbage, jalapeños and tomato.

Serve with your favorite hot sauce and extra hot pepper flakes.

> **TWEAK THE HEAT:** You can easily heat things up with extra hot pepper flakes and extra jalapeño pepper slices or your favorite hot sauce, of course.

PREP
TIME

10 minutes

COOKING
TIME

15 minutes

MAKES

4 sandwiches

HEAT
LEVEL

Medium

Southwest-Style Cheesesteak
SANDWICHES

This recipe is a riff on one of my favorite sandwiches, the Philly Cheesesteak—a thinly sliced, sautéed rib eye topped with melted cheese and sautéed bell peppers and onions served on a sandwich roll. In South Philly, they prefer Cheez Whiz for the melt factor. This version brings in some heat with salsa con queso, hotter peppers and more seasonings. I think it beats the original.

1½ lb (681 g) rib eye steak

1 tsp chili powder

1 tsp garlic powder

Salt and pepper to taste

2 tbsp (30 ml) olive oil, divided

3 large jalapeño peppers, sliced or chopped

1 large poblano pepper, sliced or chopped

1 large white onion, sliced or chopped

8 oz (227 g) salsa con queso, plus more as desired

4 large sandwich rolls, warmed, for serving

Slice the rib eye into very thin strips (it helps if the steak is slightly frozen). Season the strips with chili powder, garlic powder, salt and pepper. Set it aside for now.

In a large pan, heat a tablespoon (15 ml) of olive oil over medium heat. Add the jalapeños, poblano and onion and sauté them for 10 minutes, until they are softened and begin to caramelize.

When the peppers and onions are nearly done, heat another pan to medium heat and add the remaining olive oil. Add in the sliced rib eye steak and sauté for about a minute, or until the steak is cooked through. It should cook up very quickly. Add the salsa con queso and stir just to warm it through.

Serve the cheesesteak in warmed sandwich rolls, then top with sautéed peppers and onions.

TWEAK THE HEAT: Jalapeños are an absolute must for this recipe, but you can add more heat by introducing spicier peppers and more chili powder. Chili flakes are always welcomed, and this sandwich loves a good dose of your favorite hot sauce. Also, if you're able to get your hands on Hatch peppers, which are grown in the Hatch region of New Mexico, use them instead of the poblanos.

Buffalo Chicken
SLOPPY JOES

I grew up on canned sloppy joes and still find them enjoyable today, although modified into a homemade recipe. This version gives this childhood favorite a new spin by incorporating the flavor of Buffalo chicken. It's super tasty, and super easy to make.

2 tbsp (30 ml) olive oil

1 medium onion, chopped

3–4 spicy chili peppers, chopped

2 cloves garlic, chopped

1½ lbs (681 g) ground chicken

3 tbsp (45 g) brown sugar

2 tbsp (30 ml) Worcestershire sauce

2 tbsp (14 g) cayenne powder

1 tbsp (7 g) paprika

Salt and pepper to taste

1 cup (225 g) tomato sauce

1 cup (225 g) Buffalo sauce

2 tbsp (30 ml) apple cider vinegar

Buns, for serving

In a large pan, heat the oil over medium heat. Add the onion and chili peppers. Cook for about 5 minutes, until soft. Add the garlic and cook for another minute, stirring. Add the ground chicken and cook for about 5 minutes, stirring often, until the meat is cooked through.

Stir in the brown sugar, Worcestershire sauce, cayenne, paprika, salt and pepper, tomato sauce, Buffalo sauce and apple cider vinegar. Stir and simmer for 5 minutes to bring the flavors together. If your sauce is too thin, cook it for a bit longer to thicken.

Serve on your favorite buns.

TWEAK THE HEAT: There are various Buffalo sauces on the market, so choose one to fit your personal heat level and flavor. You can also make your own Buffalo-style sauce by combining your favorite Louisiana-style hot sauce with butter. Warm them in a pan together and use as desired.

PREP TIME

10 minutes

COOKING TIME

15 minutes

MAKES

4 large sandwiches

HEAT LEVEL

Medium-Hot

PREP
TIME

10 minutes

COOKING
TIME

20 minutes

MAKES

4 sandwiches

HEAT
LEVEL

Medium

Spinach Gouda Melt
WITH GOCHUJANG

It's hard not to love a good melt, which is essentially a grilled cheese with extra ingredients. Here, I add lightly sautéed spinach and gochujang to spice it up. Gochujang is a spicy chili paste, a bit like sriracha, but not quite as sweet. It's hard to believe this recipe is vegetarian.

FOR THE SLAW

2 large green apples, thinly sliced

1 large red bell pepper, thinly sliced

2 tbsp (28 g) mayonnaise

2 tbsp (30 g) Mexican crema or sour cream

1 tbsp (15 ml) apple cider vinegar

1 tbsp (14 g) gochujang

1 tbsp (15 ml) of your favorite hot sauce

Salt and pepper to taste

FOR THE SANDWICH

8 slices sourdough bread

2 tsp (9 g) butter, for spreading

1 tbsp (15 ml) olive oil

2 jalapeño peppers, diced

16 oz (450 g) spinach

8 slices Gouda cheese (smoked Gouda is GREAT for this)

4 tsp (16 g) gochujang, for serving

To make the slaw, toss the green apples and red bell pepper into a bowl with the mayonnaise, crema, vinegar, gochujang, hot sauce and a pinch of salt and pepper. Make sure to coat everything evenly. Refrigerate until the sandwiches are done.

Next, preheat your oven to 350°F (180°C). Heat a large pan to medium heat. Butter the bread slices and set them butter-side down in the pan for a couple of minutes, until they get toasty and start to brown. Set them onto a large baking sheet.

In the same pan, add the olive oil and jalapeño peppers. Cook them for 5 minutes, stirring occasionally. Then, add the spinach and cook for another 5 minutes or so, until the spinach softens up.

Pile the spinach-jalapeño mix on 4 of the bread slices, then top them with a couple slices of cheese. Put them in the oven to bake for 5 to 10 minutes, or until the cheese is nice and melty.

Top each slice with the spicy slaw. Squeeze some more of the gochujang and top with the remaining slices of toasted bread.

TWEAK THE HEAT: You can adjust your spiciness by using more or less of the gochujang. Also, consider adding spicier peppers to the slaw for some extra kick.

Chicago-Style
MEATBALL SUBS WITH SPICY GIARDINIERA

I grew up in the Chicago area, where you can get a good meatball sub just about anywhere. I consider myself spoiled! Chicago has some distinctive dishes that I'd truly miss if I ever moved away. Luckily, though, this particular version of the recipe will go with me wherever I go.

PREP TIME

15 minutes

COOKING TIME

20 minutes

MAKES

4 sandwiches

HEAT LEVEL

Medium–Hot

FOR THE GIARDINIERA SAUCE

1 tbsp (15 ml) olive oil

¼ cup (38 g) chopped onion

¼ cup (45 g) chopped sweet pepper

1 clove garlic, chopped

1 (12-oz [340-g]) can tomato sauce

2 tbsp (26 g) hot giardiniera, plus more for serving

1 tsp dried oregano

Pinch of sugar

Salt and pepper to taste

FOR THE MEATBALLS

12 oz (340 g) ground beef

12 oz (340 g) spicy Italian sausage

1 cup (175 g) chopped sweet peppers

1 small onion, chopped

3 cloves garlic, chopped

1 egg

½ cup (30 g) Italian bread crumbs, or more as needed

Warmed Italian buns and shredded provolone, for serving

Preheat the oven to 400°F (200°C).

To make the sauce, heat the oil in a small pot set to medium heat. Then, add the onion and sweet pepper and cook for about 4 to 5 minutes, until soft. Add the garlic and cook another minute. Add the tomato sauce, giardiniera, oregano, sugar and salt and pepper. Simmer for at least 15 minutes. The flavor will broaden the longer you simmer the sauce.

In a large bowl, add the ground beef, Italian sausage, sweet peppers, onion, garlic, egg and bread crumbs. Hand mix, but do not overmix or the meatballs will become mealy.

Form the meat mixture into 16 meatballs, about 1½ ounces (43 g) each. Set them onto a baking sheet and bake them for 12 to 15 minutes, or until they are cooked through.

Add 4 meatballs per sandwich, then top with your red sauce and provolone cheese. Bake for about 5 minutes in order to melt the cheese.

Garnish with extra giardiniera.

TWEAK THE HEAT: Hot giardiniera is typically available at your local grocer. It is essentially a mixture of lightly brined peppers and vegetables that have been preserved in olive oil or, sometimes, a vinaigrette. I always go for the hot variety, which packs a bit of heat, though there are also milder versions available.

PREP
TIME

10 minutes

COOKING
TIME

5 minutes

MAKES

4 po' boy
sandwiches

HEAT
LEVEL

MEDIUM

Pan-Seared Shrimp
PO' BOYS WITH SPICY CHILI RÉMOULADE

Whenever we visit New Orleans, we always make it a point to get a famous po' boy sandwich. The story is, they were created in the 1920s to inexpensively feed men on strike, who were jokingly referred to as "poor boys." They are typically served with fried shrimp or oysters, and "dressed" with mayonnaise, lettuce, tomato and pickle. This is my spicier version.

FOR THE SHRIMP
1 lb (454 g) shrimp, peeled and deveined
1 tbsp (15 ml) olive oil
2 tbsp (24 g) Cajun seasoning

4 lightly toasted French rolls or buns, sliced jalapeño peppers, sliced cucumber and sliced tomato, for serving

FOR THE RÉMOULADE
½ cup (112 g) mayonnaise
3 tbsp (48 g) spicy brown mustard
2 tbsp (30 ml) Louisiana-style hot sauce
1 tsp Cajun seasoning
1 jalapeño pepper, chopped
1 clove garlic, chopped

In a large bowl, toss the shrimp with the olive oil and Cajun seasoning blend. Heat a large pan to medium heat and add the shrimp. Cook them for a couple of minutes on each side, until they are cooked through.

Stack the cooked shrimp on the toasted French rolls. Then, top with sliced jalapeños, cucumber and tomato.

Make the rémoulade by adding the mayonnaise, brown mustard, hot sauce, Cajun seasoning, jalapeño and garlic to a food processor and processing until smooth. Pour it over the sandwiches.

TWEAK THE HEAT: Cajun seasoning offers up a good level of flavor, and you'll get a bit of heat from the jalapeño pepper in the rémoulade. If you're looking to up that heat level, consider adding more jalapeño, or going with hotter peppers, like the serrano or even the fiery habanero. Dial back on the jalapeño and seasoning for a milder version.

Piquant Pasta!

Pasta is one of the easiest ways to get dinner on the table in no time. Almost every recipe here should take about 30 minutes, give or take. You can boil some pasta in a flash, leaving you time to build up some of those spicy flavors we all crave. Pasta is ideal for soaking up savory sauces, and it loves bold ingredients.

You'll certainly see a lot of Italian influence in these recipes, as pasta is practically defined by Italy, and the Italians know what they're doing when it comes to making great food. However, I've included some recipes that are more like adaptations with a southern influence.

They're all pretty spicy, though like all of my recipes, you can easily adjust the heat and spice level to your preference.

PREP
TIME

10 minutes

COOKING
TIME

30 minutes

SERVES

4

HEAT
LEVEL

Medium-Hot

Pasta Carbonara with
HOT ITALIAN SAUSAGE

I fell in love with carbonara in Italy and was beside myself when I found out how easy it is to prepare. At its core, it is pasta with pancetta (Italian bacon), Parmesan cheese and eggs. The eggs cook in the hot pasta, making it a very silky sauce. Here is my version of pasta carbonara with a spicy twist.

1 tsp olive oil

4 spicy Italian sausage links

8 oz (227 g) pasta noodles (I used orecchiette noodles)

4 slices bacon (or pancetta), chopped

1 small sweet onion, chopped

2 hot red peppers, chopped (I used cayenne peppers)

4 tbsp (57 g) unsalted butter, cubed

⅓ cup (60 g) grated Parmesan cheese, plus more for serving

1 handful fresh basil leaves

2 large eggs, beaten

Salt and pepper to taste

Pinch of crushed red pepper

Juice from 1 lemon

Cherry tomatoes, for serving

In a large pan set to medium heat, heat the oil. Add the sausages and cook for 12 to 15 minutes, flipping often, until they are cooked through. Remove them from the pan and slice them. Set them aside for now.

Bring a pot of salted water to a boil and cook the noodles until al dente, about 10 minutes. Drain them, but keep ½ cup (120 ml) of the pasta water.

In the pan with the sausages, add the chopped bacon, onion and peppers. Cook them for 6 minutes, until the bacon is cooked through.

Add the pasta water and the butter. Stir and let it simmer for a couple of minutes, until the liquid has reduced a bit.

Toss in the pasta and grated Parmesan cheese and stir. Stir in the sliced Italian sausage and fresh basil. Remove the pan from the heat and quickly stir in the beaten eggs. The hot pasta will cook the eggs through. Be sure to stir quickly or the eggs will start to set.

Give the whole pan a pinch or two of salt and black pepper. Sprinkle with red pepper flakes and squeeze some lemon juice over the top.

Serve with cherry tomatoes and extra Parmesan cheese.

HOT TIP: If you have a hard time finding fresh basil, spinach leaves make a tasty alternative. You can also drizzle your favorite olive oil over the top of your plate for a nice flavor pop.

Spicy Chili–Almond Pesto
WITH SOFT-BOILED EGG

Pesto is a gift from the heavens. Bold statement, I know. The combination of quality olive oil, fresh basil, salty Parmesan cheese and nuts is unrivaled. Best of all, it is ridiculously easy to make. My variation adds a bit of heat to the mix with fresh and dried peppers to satisfy our spiciness quotient.

PREP TIME

10 minutes

COOKING TIME

10 minutes

SERVES

4

HEAT LEVEL

Medium

1 cup (25 g) packed fresh basil

1 jalapeño pepper, chopped

1 clove garlic, chopped

¼ cup (30 g) chopped almonds

¼ cup (45 g) shredded Parmesan cheese, plus more for serving

1 tsp red chili flakes, plus more for serving

Pinch of cracked black pepper, plus more for serving

½ cup (120 ml) olive oil

8 oz (227 g) pasta noodles

4 large eggs

Fresh chopped parsley and sliced tomato, for serving

In a food processor, add the basil, jalapeño, garlic, almonds, Parmesan cheese, chili flakes and a pinch of black pepper. Process until it is nice and chunky. Drizzle in the olive oil a bit at a time and process until incorporated. The pesto should be smooth. Set aside.

In a large pot, boil the pasta in salted water until al dente, about 10 minutes. Drain and toss the noodles in a large bowl with the pesto. Make sure all the noodles are coated.

In a separate pot, gently lower the eggs into boiling salted water. Boil for 6 minutes. Drain and cool before peeling.

Serve the pasta in bowls and garnish with extra Parmesan cheese, extra black pepper, chili flakes, fresh parsley and tomato slices. Top with sliced soft-boiled eggs.

HOT TIP: Traditional pesto is made with pine nuts, which are fatty and delicious, but also quite expensive. Almonds are a great alternative, but you can also use other nuts, like walnuts, or even sunflower seeds. Feel free to experiment.

TWEAK THE HEAT: Extra chili flakes are a simple way to spice this dish up even more, though spicier peppers in the pesto can really ramp things up, as well as a few extra grinds of black pepper.

PREP
TIME

10 minutes

COOKING
TIME

5 minutes

SERVES

4

HEAT
LEVEL

Hot

Habanero–Pecan–Parsley
PESTO GNOCCHI

This pesto variation brings in the mighty heat of the habanero for a dish that will REALLY elevate the zest factor. While traditional pesto incorporates pine nuts and fresh basil, we're swapping in pecans and parsley for a version that is a bit more accessible. I like to make my own gnocchi and freeze it for easy meals, but you can easily grab some from the grocer.

1 cup (60 g) packed fresh parsley

1 habanero pepper, chopped

2 cloves garlic, chopped

¾ cup (95 g) chopped pecans, divided

¼ cup (45 g) shredded Parmesan cheese, plus more for serving

1 tsp red chili flakes, plus more for serving

Pinch of cracked black pepper, plus more for serving

½ cup (120 ml) olive oil

16 oz (454 g) prepared gnocchi

4 oz (113 g) soppressata, sliced

Fresh chopped basil and sliced tomato, for serving

In a food processor, add the parsley, habanero, garlic, ¼ cup (30 g) of pecans, Parmesan cheese, chili flakes and a few pinches of black pepper. Process until it is nice and chunky. Drizzle in the olive oil a bit at a time and process until incorporated. The pesto should be smooth. Set aside.

Bring a pot of lightly salted water to a boil. Add the gnocchi and boil for 4 to 5 minutes, or until they start to float. Drain and toss the gnocchi in a large bowl with the pesto. Make sure all the gnocchi are nicely coated.

In a small pan, heat the soppressata slices and ½ cup (65 g) of pecans, until the soppressata begins to release its oils, about 3 to 4 minutes. Remove from the heat and toss with the gnocchi and pesto.

Serve the gnocchi in bowls and garnish with extra Parmesan cheese, chili flakes, fresh basil, tomato slices and black pepper.

TWEAK THE HEAT: You will get PLENTY of heat with the habanero pepper, but if you feel it is pushing your limits, feel free to substitute it with a milder pepper, such as a cayenne or even a sweet pepper for a "zero heat" version. If you're like me and want a bit more heat, toss in another habanero.

Fiery Shrimp Scampi
WITH HABANEROS

I was well into my twenties the first time I tried shrimp scampi. My then future wife brought me to a local Italian place whose specialty was scampi, so I gave it a try. Wow! Talk about flavor! At its core, scampi sauce is butter, white wine, lemon juice and garlic. The butter thickens as you warm it and cooks the shrimp to perfection. This version uses extra garlic and habaneros to suit my spicy needs.

PREP TIME

15 minutes

COOKING TIME

15 minutes

SERVES

4

HEAT LEVEL

Hot

1 lb (454 g) shrimp, peeled and deveined

3 tbsp (45 ml) olive oil, divided, plus more as needed

2 habanero peppers, chopped, plus more for serving

1 tbsp (8 g) spicy chili flakes, plus more for serving

1 tsp paprika

1 tsp garlic powder

Salt and pepper to taste

6 cloves garlic, minced

Juice from ½ lemon

¼ cup (60 ml) white wine

½ stick butter

Cooked angel hair pasta (about 8 oz [227 g]), chopped fresh parsley and shredded Parmesan cheese, for serving

Dry the shrimp with paper towels, then toss them in a bowl with a tablespoon (15 ml) of olive oil, the habaneros, chili flakes, paprika, garlic powder, salt and pepper. Set them in the refrigerator for 10 minutes to let the flavors permeate the shrimp.

Heat a large pan to medium heat and add the other 2 tablespoons (30 ml) of the olive oil. Add the shrimp and cook them with the habaneros for a minute on each side. Remove the habanero peppers and the shrimp from the pan and set aside for now. Reserve the oil.

Add the garlic to the oiled pan. If you feel you need a bit more oil, add in a teaspoon or so. Cook the garlic for a minute, until fragrant.

Stir in the lemon juice and white wine. Cook it for a couple minutes to let it reduce slightly. Add the butter and swirl until melted. Let the sauce simmer until thickened, about 5 minutes.

Add the shrimp and simmer for a couple more minutes until the shrimp is completely cooked through. Serve with freshly cooked angel hair pasta topped with fresh parsley, Parmesan cheese, extra chili flakes and extra chopped habanero, if desired.

TWEAK THE HEAT: The habanero peppers and chili flakes will give you a double whammy of heat, first in the buttery sauce, then in the fresh pop on top of the pasta. You can reduce the heat by dialing back on the habanero peppers. Just include some in the initial sauce and skip the chili flakes. Or, go with milder peppers. Sweet peppers work great for this recipe.

For a hotter version, feel free to add in more habanero peppers.

Creamy Cajun Chicken and
ANDOUILLE PASTA

PREP
TIME

10 minutes

COOKING
TIME

20 minutes

SERVES

4

HEAT
LEVEL

Medium

Every now and then I like to bring a Cajun twist to my pasta dishes. This recipe swaps out traditional Italian herbs for your favorite Cajun seasoning blend and adds chicken and smoked andouille sausage. It's sort of a mashup—pasta meets gumbo. Definitely one of my favorites.

1 tbsp (15 ml) olive oil

10 oz (283 g) chicken breast, cut into strips

3 tbsp (36 g) Cajun seasoning, divided

8 oz (227 g) smoked andouille sausage, sliced

1 small onion, chopped

1 stalk celery, chopped

2–3 jalapeño peppers, chopped

3 cloves garlic, chopped

6 oz (170 g) tomato paste

1 cup (240 ml) chicken stock

¼ cup (60 g) Mexican crema or sour cream

8–10 oz (227–283 g) prepared pasta noodles (I used farfalle)

Extra pan-seared jalapeño peppers (optional), sliced cherry tomatoes, lemon and hot sauce, for serving

In a large pan, heat the oil to medium heat. Season the chicken with a tablespoon (12 g) of Cajun seasoning, then add it to the pan with the andouille, onion, celery and jalapeños. Cook them for 4 to 5 minutes, or until the onion, celery and jalapeños soften up and the chicken starts to cook through.

Add the garlic and cook another minute, until fragrant.

Add the tomato paste, chicken stock and remaining Cajun seasoning. Stir until sauce-like, 3 to 4 minutes. Reduce the heat to low and let it simmer for 15 minutes or so to let the flavors develop.

Remove the sauce from the heat and swirl in the crema. Then, add the pasta noodles.

Serve in bowls and top with extra jalapeño peppers and sliced cherry tomatoes. It is GREAT with a bit of squeezed lemon over the top. Don't forget the hot sauce.

HOT TIP: You can use heavy cream if you'd like a very creamy version of this recipe. Cream cheese works great as well, though I find that crema or sour cream adds just the right amount of creaminess, without adding too many calories.

TWEAK THE HEAT: If you're looking for a spicier version, feel free to go heavy on the Cajun seasoning, and don't be shy with the hot sauce. I prefer a thick Louisiana style.

Loaded Taco Pasta

Give your "Taco Tuesday" a pasta twist with this recipe. If you're like me, you always have taco seasoning on hand. I like to make my own custom seasoning blends, but I still find it convenient to buy large containers of the blend for quick and convenient meals. You'll love this Italian–Mexican mashup.

1 tbsp (15 ml) olive oil
1 small onion, chopped
1 jalapeño pepper, chopped
1 poblano pepper, chopped
1 serrano pepper, chopped
3 cloves garlic, chopped
1 lb (454 g) ground beef

4 tbsp (28 g) of your favorite taco seasoning
½ cup (120 ml) water, or more as needed
8–10 oz (227–283 g) prepared pasta noodles (I used elbow macaroni)
Extra pan-seared jalapeño peppers (if desired), sliced cherry tomatoes, fresh cilantro, shredded cheddar cheese, lime juice, chili flakes and hot sauce, for serving

In a large pan, heat the oil to medium heat. Add the onion and peppers. Cook them for 4 to 5 minutes, or until they start to soften up. Add the garlic and cook another minute, until fragrant.

Add the ground beef and break it apart with a wooden spoon. Cook it down for about 5 minutes, until the meat is mostly cooked through.

Stir in the taco seasoning and water, then reduce the heat to low. Simmer for 15 minutes to let the flavors develop. You can simmer longer if you'd like. If the meat mixture looks too dry, add a bit more water.

While the meat is simmering, boil the noodles in salt water for about 10 minutes. Combine the noodles with the meat mixture and remove the pan from the heat.

Serve in bowls and top with extra jalapeño peppers (if desired), sliced cherry tomatoes, fresh cilantro, shredded cheddar cheese, lime juice, chili flakes and hot sauce.

HOT TIP: Feel free to include other traditional taco toppings with this dish, like black olives, sliced avocado or crumbly white cheese.

TWEAK THE HEAT: If you'd like a spicier version, you can easily go heavier on the taco seasoning—add another tablespoon or two (7 or 14 g)—and opt for more jalapeño or serrano peppers.

PREP
TIME

10 minutes

COOKING
TIME

25 minutes

SERVES

4

HEAT
LEVEL

Mild

Pasta with Smoked ANDOUILLE, PEPPERS AND COLLARD GREENS

I got hooked on collard greens while visiting the South, where greens are commonly served. They are fibrous and tough when raw, but when cooked right, they are juicy and fall apart in your mouth. This pasta dish incorporates the classic combination of collard greens and smoked andouille, with a good helping of peppers, of course.

3 strips bacon, chopped

1 medium yellow onion, chopped

3-4 sweet peppers, chopped

3 cloves garlic, chopped

1 bunch collard greens, stemmed and chopped (about 8 oz [227 g])

8 oz (227 g) smoked andouille, sliced

½ cup (120 ml) chicken broth

Salt and pepper to taste

Spicy chili flakes, plus more for serving (optional)

8 oz (227 g) cooked pasta

¼ cup (45 g) grated Parmesan cheese, plus more for serving

Heat a large pan to medium heat and add the bacon. Cook for a couple of minutes, until the fat begins to render. Add the onion and chopped peppers. Stir and cook for about 5 minutes, until soft.

Add the garlic and cook until fragrant. Add the chopped greens in 2 batches and stir. Cook them for a couple of minutes, or until wilted.

Add in the andouille sausage, chicken broth, some salt and pepper and a pinch of spicy chili flakes (optional). Cover and cook for about 15 minutes.

Stir in the cooked pasta and Parmesan cheese. Serve in bowls and sprinkle with extra Parmesan and spicy chili flakes.

TWEAK THE HEAT: This recipe isn't meant to be overly spicy. Instead, the juicy collard greens and smoky andouille sausage make it huge on flavor. If you're looking for something hotter, you can easily add in extra spicy chili flakes, or substitute the sweeter peppers for a hot pepper, such as a jalapeño or cayenne.

Cheesy Hot Sausage and
TORTELLINI SKILLET WITH THREE PEPPERS

My wife absolutely LOVES tortellini. We enjoy making pasta at home, and she invariably chooses either ravioli or tortellini. There is something so ultimately satisfying about soft pasta filled with cheeses or meats that melt in your mouth. You don't have to make homemade pasta, though, to enjoy a good tortellini. There are a number of great brands available through your grocer for quick and easy meals. I thought this recipe was more medium-hot, but my wife said it was VERY HOT, so I'm listing it in the middle. Like all the recipes in this book, it's easy to adjust to your preferences.

PREP TIME

5 minutes

COOKING TIME

25 minutes

SERVES

4

HEAT LEVEL

Hot

1 tsp olive oil

1 lb (454 g) Italian sausage

1 large jalapeño pepper, chopped

1 serrano pepper, chopped

1 medium sweet pepper, chopped

1 small yellow onion, chopped

3 cloves garlic, chopped

2 (14-oz [397-g]) cans tomato sauce

1 tbsp (5 g) dried oregano

1 tsp smoked paprika

1 tsp crushed red pepper, plus more for serving

Salt and pepper to taste

12 oz (340 g) cooked cheese-filled tortellini

¾ cup (112 g) cherry tomatoes (optional)

1 cup (130 g) shredded Monterey Jack cheese (or mozzarella)

Fresh chopped basil, for serving

Heat a large pan to medium heat and add the olive oil. Add the Italian sausage, peppers and onion. Cook them down for 5 minutes, stirring and breaking apart the sausage.

Add the garlic and cook until fragrant. Add the tomato sauce, oregano, paprika, crushed red pepper and a bit of salt and pepper. Stir and reduce the heat to a simmer. Simmer for 15 minutes.

While the sauce is cooking, prepare the tortellini according to the packaging instructions. Drain and toss the cooked tortellini and cherry tomatoes into the sauce. Cook for a minute, stirring.

Add the cheese and cover for a minute or two, until the cheese has nicely melted.

Garnish with fresh chopped basil and extra crushed red pepper.

TWEAK THE HEAT: Hot Italian sausage can be quite spicy, especially when paired with serranos, jalapeños and hot pepper flakes. You can easily dial back the heat factor by using a milder sausage and omitting the serranos, which are the hottest of the trio. Add in more sweet peppers or an extra jalapeño for a mid-range heat level, and go easy on the pepper flakes.

For a hotter version, you can easily include more pepper flakes and introduce a hotter chili powder, such as cayenne or even smoked ghost chili powder.

All-the-Way Arrabbiata

"Arrabbiata" in Italian translates to "angry," so you know your taste buds are in for a ride. The sauce is traditionally made with tomatoes, garlic and chili flakes cooked in olive oil. The "angry" bits come from the heat of the chili flakes. This version includes fresh ghost peppers as well as ghost pepper flakes, if you so dare. Remember, you can easily tame the heat with milder peppers. This dish is not for the faint of heart.

PREP TIME

5 minutes

COOKING TIME

25 minutes

SERVES

4

HEAT LEVEL

Very Hot

1 tbsp (15 ml) olive oil, plus more for serving

1 small onion, chopped

1 ghost pepper, chopped (optional for REAL heat)

2 red Fresno peppers, chopped

3 cloves garlic, crushed

1 tsp ghost pepper flakes, plus more for serving (for a milder substitution, use crushed red pepper flakes)

1 (14-oz [397-g]) can diced tomatoes

¾ cup (130 g) cherry tomatoes

4 oz (113 g) hot soppressata, chopped

Salt and pepper to taste

1 lb (454 g) pasta noodles (I used penne)

Fresh chopped basil, for serving

Heat a large pan to medium heat and add the olive oil. Add the onion, ghost pepper and Fresno peppers. Cook them down for 5 minutes, or until soft.

Add the garlic and pepper flakes; stir to coat. Cook until fragrant, about a minute.

Add the diced tomatoes, cherry tomatoes and hot soppressata. Season with salt and pepper. Stir and reduce the heat to a simmer. Simmer for 15 minutes.

While the sauce is cooking, prepare your noodles according to the packaging instructions. Drain, but reserve about a cup (240 ml) of the pasta water. Stir a half cup (120 ml) of the pasta water into the sauce to loosen it up. Stir in more pasta water, if needed.

Stir in the noodles, then garnish with fresh chopped basil and extra pepper flakes. Drizzle with extra olive oil and serve.

HOT TIP: This isn't an overly saucy recipe. If you'd like a saucier version, stir in another can of diced tomatoes or tomato sauce.

TWEAK THE HEAT: This recipe brings some serious heat. If you haven't cooked with ghost peppers, prepare yourself. For a milder version, you can easily swap out ghost peppers for other peppers. Habaneros will bring a very nice level of heat. You can usually find ghost pepper flakes online, though I like to grow my own and dehydrate them at home.

Blazing Breakfasts
(for Dinner)

If I could eat breakfast for dinner every day of the week, I would! It's the same with my wife. There is something fun about mixing up your meals, and whipping up a batch of eggs or French toast in the evening. Many breakfasts are simple to prepare, so they're sort of a no-brainer for busy people who enjoy good food.

Breakfast food takes to spiciness in the best of ways. You can incorporate all sorts of chili peppers, seasonings, sauces and more to bring in that zest factor we all crave.

These are some of my favorite breakfast recipes, each with a savory spin to make them more appropriate for a dinner setting, though they could easily be served for brunch. We've got jacked-up hash, waffles, French toast, eggs, omelets and so much more.

PREP TIME
10 minutes
COOKING TIME
30 minutes
SERVES
4
HEAT LEVEL
Medium

Jacked-Up
BREAKFAST HASH

There is nothing like a hearty hash to stick to your bones, so why relegate it to breakfast alone? Packed with potatoes, bacon, smoked turkey, chilies and lots of seasoning, this will make for a satisfying dinner any night of the week.

2 strips thick-cut bacon, diced

1 lb (454 g) potatoes, diced

Salt and pepper to taste

1 red bell pepper, diced

3 jalapeño peppers, diced

10 oz (283 g) smoked turkey breast, diced

2 tbsp (18 g) red chili powder (I used morita powder)

1 tsp garlic powder

4 eggs

Pinch of spicy chili flakes

Chopped parsley, crumbly white cheese, limes and hot sauce, for serving

Heat a large pan to medium heat and add the bacon. Stir and cook for about 5 minutes to render the fat. Add the potatoes and stir. Add in a pinch of salt and cook for about 10 minutes. The potatoes will start to crisp up around the edges.

Next, add in the red bell pepper, jalapeño peppers, diced smoked turkey, chili powder, garlic powder and a bit of salt and pepper. Stir and cook for 5 minutes.

With a wooden spoon, make 4 indentations in the cooking mixture and crack 1 egg in each. Season with a bit of salt and pepper. Cook for about 5 minutes, or until the egg whites cook through. Sprinkle with the spicy chili flakes.

Remove from the heat and cool slightly. Top with the fresh parsley and crumbly white cheese. Squeeze a bit of lime juice over the hash and serve with hot sauce.

> **HOT TIP:** I enjoy smoked turkey with this recipe, but if you have difficulty finding it, you can easily skip it and include more bacon instead, or smoked ham.

> **TWEAK THE HEAT:** Looking for a spicier version? Add more jalapeño peppers or try spicier peppers, like serranos or cayenne. You can also add more chili powder. I used red morita chili powder, but you can use any store-bought blend. Also, consider using spicy chorizo instead of bacon and turkey for an even zestier version.
>
> Looking for a milder version? Cut back on the jalapeño peppers and use a green bell pepper instead.

Chilaquiles Verdes

Chilaquiles is a traditional Mexican dish made with crispy tortillas that are drenched in a green or red sauce. It is typically served for breakfast or brunch. This is a green version made with an easy-to-make salsa verde.

PREP TIME

10 minutes

COOKING TIME

20 minutes

SERVES

4

HEAT LEVEL

Medium

FOR THE SALSA VERDE

1½ lbs (681 g) tomatillos, sliced

2 jalapeño peppers, chopped

4 cloves garlic

1 small red onion, chopped

2 tbsp (2 g) chopped cilantro, plus more for serving

¼ cup (60 ml) white wine vinegar

Juice from 1 lime

Salt to taste

FOR THE CHILAQUILES

1 (13-oz [368-g]) bag tortilla chips

1 tbsp (15 ml) olive oil

4 large eggs

Sliced avocado, sliced jalapeño pepper, lime wedges and queso fresco, for serving

In a food processor, add the tomatillos, jalapeño peppers, garlic, red onion, cilantro, white wine vinegar, lime juice and salt to make the salsa verde. Process until you achieve a nice, smooth sauce. Pour it into a large pan and heat it gently through, about 20 minutes. Taste and adjust for salt. Add the tortilla chips and toss to coat.

In a separate large pan, heat a tablespoon (15 ml) of olive oil and add the eggs. Fry them for about 4 minutes, or until the whites have set.

Serve the eggs over the tortilla chips in the pan, or first distribute the chilaquiles to plates and top with the eggs.

Garnish with avocado, jalapeño peppers, lime wedges, queso fresco and chopped fresh cilantro.

HOT TIPS: If you leave the tortilla chips in the pan with the sauce, they will begin to soften. Some people prefer their chips soggy. It depends on your preference.

Consider adding shredded chicken for a dinner version of this meal.

TWEAK THE HEAT: To up the heat factor, you can easily include more jalapeño or even introduce something spicier, such as a serrano pepper, fiery chili flakes or your favorite hot sauce.

PREP
TIME

10 minutes

COOKING
TIME

15 to 20
minutes

MAKES

6 (7-inch
[18-cm])
waffles

HEAT
LEVEL

Medium

Cheesy Chipotle Cheddar
WAFFLES WITH AVOCADO CREMA

As much as I love a good sweet waffle, I would choose savory over sweet any time. Waffle batter is super easy to whip together and it is very versatile, since it's able to absorb any number of additional ingredients. This recipe incorporates tangy chipotle sauce as well as spicy serrano peppers and cheddar cheese.

FOR THE WAFFLE BATTER
2 large eggs
1¾ cups (429 ml) buttermilk
8 tbsp (112 g) melted butter
1 cup (121 g) shredded cheddar cheese
2 serrano peppers, chopped
1 (7-oz [198-g]) can chipotle sauce, divided
1 cup (120 g) all-purpose flour
1 cup (150 g) cornmeal
2 tsp (7 g) baking powder
1 tsp baking soda
1 tsp salt
1 tbsp (20 g) honey

FOR THE AVOCADO CREMA
1 small avocado, peeled and pitted
1 cup (240 g) Mexican crema or sour cream
1 tbsp (1 g) chopped cilantro
1 tbsp (20 g) honey
Salt and pepper to taste

Diced avocado, sliced serrano peppers and tomato, for serving

Spray the waffle iron with a nonstick cooking spray and preheat it.

In a large mixing bowl, beat together the eggs, buttermilk and melted butter. Stir in the cheese, serrano peppers and half the can of chipotle sauce. Reserve the other half.

In a separate bowl, stir together the all-purpose flour, cornmeal, baking powder, baking soda and salt. Combine the wet and dry ingredients, stirring just until fairly smooth; it's OK if it is still lumpy.

In a small pan, pour the other half of the chipotle sauce and swirl in a tablespoon (20 g) of honey. Heat it until it is slightly warm and set aside.

In a food processor, add the avocado, crema, cilantro, honey and salt and pepper to make the avocado crema. Process until it is nice and smooth. Set it aside.

Pour the waffle mix in the waffle iron as needed and cook for 2 to 4 minutes, until cooked to your desired consistency. Remove and set on a plate. Drizzle with avocado crema and sweet chipotle sauce. Serve with avocado, serrano peppers and tomato.

TWEAK THE HEAT: You can omit the serrano peppers for a milder version of this recipe, or go with hotter peppers. You can add in any of your favorite complimentary seasonings, such as chipotle powder, chili powder, Cajun blend or even taco seasoning. Try it out with your favorite hot sauce. Happy experimenting!

Chorizo con Huevos with POTATO AND BLACK BEANS

I sometimes order chorizo con huevos (eggs with chorizo) for lunch at my favorite Mexican restaurant. When they see me walking in, they automatically toss a few jalapeño peppers on the grill. It's a simple dish, made with crumbly Mexican chorizo and scrambled eggs, served on warmed tortillas. This is a version I like to make at home with a few extra seasonings and ingredients.

PREP TIME

10 minutes

COOKING TIME

15 minutes

SERVES

4

HEAT LEVEL

Medium–Hot

1 tbsp (15 ml) olive oil

1 medium potato, diced

1 small onion, chopped

1 jalapeño pepper, chopped

6 oz (170 g) Mexican chorizo

3–4 small, spicy chili peppers, left whole (see the notes below)

2 cloves garlic, chopped

2 tbsp (18 g) chili powder (or use a taco seasoning blend)

1 tsp cumin

Salt and pepper to taste

6 large eggs, beaten

1 (15-oz [420-g]) can black beans, drained

Fresh chopped cilantro, sliced avocado, crumbly white cheese, warmed tortillas, lime wedges and hot sauce, for serving

Heat a large pan to medium heat and add the oil. Add the potato, onion, jalapeño and chorizo. Cook for about 6 to 7 minutes, or until the chorizo breaks down and cooks through.

Add the whole chili peppers and stir. Allow them to soften for about 3 minutes

Stir in the garlic, chili powder, cumin, salt and pepper. Cook until fragrant.

Pour in the eggs and stir with a wooden spoon. Cook until the eggs have set, about 6 to 7 minutes. When the eggs are just about set, stir in the black beans and warm them.

Serve with fresh cilantro, sliced avocado, crumbly white cheese, warmed tortillas, lime wedges and your favorite hot sauce.

TWEAK THE HEAT: Look for a spicy Mexican chorizo for this recipe, though there are milder varieties if you'd like to tame the heat. For the spicy chili peppers, I found some green fingerlings at my local grocer, though feel free to choose some that satisfy your tastes, such as jalapeños or serranos, which are much easier to find.

PREP
TIME

10 minutes

COOKING
TIME

15 minutes

SERVES

4

HEAT
LEVEL

Medium

Creole–Spiced Steak and
EGGS WITH CREAMY
GOAT CHEESE POLENTA

Your typical steak and eggs dish gets a makeover with spicy Creole seasoning and a creamy polenta enriched with goat cheese. Polenta cooks up in a flash, as does the thinly sliced rib eye. You'll have this meal on the table in well under 30 minutes.

1 cup (150 g) cornmeal

4 oz (113 g) goat cheese

2 tbsp (30 g) Creole seasoning, plus 1 tsp, divided

Salt and pepper to taste

3 tbsp (45 ml) olive oil, divided

4 (6-oz [170-g]) thin-cut rib eye steaks, ½" (1.3 cm) thick or thinner

1 tsp garlic powder

1 large jalapeño pepper, sliced

4–8 eggs

Fresh chopped parsley, your favorite hot sauce and cracked black pepper, for serving

Start the polenta by adding the cornmeal to a pot with 4 cups (960 ml) of water and a teaspoon of salt. Bring the water to a quick boil, then reduce the heat. Simmer for 6 to 7 minutes, until it becomes very creamy. Stir in the goat cheese and a teaspoon of the Creole seasoning. Remove the pot from the heat and swirl until all of the cheese is incorporated. Taste and adjust for salt and pepper.

Heat a large pan to medium heat and add 1 tablespoon (15 ml) olive oil. Season both sides of the steaks with the Creole seasoning, garlic powder, salt and pepper. Add the steaks and jalapeño pepper to the pan. Sear each side of the steaks for 3 to 4 minutes, or until they are done to your liking.

Spoon the creamy polenta into wide bowls and top with cracked pepper. Slice the steaks thinly and set them over the polenta. Top with the jalapeño peppers.

Heat a separate pan to medium heat and add a couple of tablespoons (30 ml) of olive oil. Lightly fry the eggs until the whites set, about 2 to 3 minutes. Serve 1 to 2 eggs per person. Set the eggs over the polenta and steaks.

Serve with fresh parsley, hot sauce and cracked black pepper.

HOT TIP: You can use thicker cuts of rib eye for this meal, but be sure to adjust your cooking time accordingly.

TWEAK THE HEAT: Feel free to adjust the Creole seasoning up or down to your personal preference. Some brands of Creole seasoning can be salty, so keep that in mind when adding salt. Add in more peppers and hot sauce for an extra kick.

Spicy Pepper Omelets with
WHIPPED GOAT CHEESE AND SWEET CHILI SAUCE

Omelets are sort of a go-to for me when I have very little time but want something substantial to eat. Eggs cook quicker than most foods and when you prepare them as an omelet, you're free to fill them up with whatever you're in the mood for. This is a particular favorite of mine, filled with creamy whipped goat cheese, avocado and plenty of spicy chili peppers.

PREP TIME

10 minutes

COOKING TIME

20 minutes

SERVES

4

HEAT LEVEL

Medium–Hot

FOR THE GOAT CHEESE AND SWEET CHILI SAUCE

6 oz (170 g) goat cheese

2 oz (57 g) Parmesan cheese, grated

1 tbsp (15 ml) heavy cream or milk

1 tsp spicy chili flakes, plus more for serving

1 tbsp (1 g) fresh chopped cilantro, plus more for garnish

Salt and pepper to taste

1 cup (245 g) sambal oelek

1 tsp honey

FOR THE OMELETS

2 tbsp (30 ml) olive oil, plus more for cooking

1 jalapeño pepper, sliced

1 serrano pepper, sliced

1 red fingerling pepper, sliced

8 eggs

2 medium-sized avocados, peeled, pitted and diced

Fresh parsley, for serving

In a food processor, add the goat cheese, Parmesan, heavy cream, spicy chili flakes, cilantro and a pinch of salt and pepper. Process until smooth and creamy. You can also do this with a fork. For fluffier cheese, add a bit more cream. Set it aside.

For the sweet chili sauce, use a small bowl to whisk together the sambal oelek and honey. Set aside.

Heat a large pan to medium heat and add 2 tablespoons (30 ml) of olive oil. Add the sliced peppers and cook them until they start to crisp up, about 5 minutes. Set them aside.

Beat 2 eggs in a small bowl. Add a teaspoon of the olive oil to the heated pan. Pour in the eggs and swirl to cover the pan.

Season the eggs with salt, pepper and chili flakes. When the eggs are nearly set, scoop in a quarter of the goat cheese mixture and a quarter of the cooked peppers. Let the eggs set, then spoon on diced avocado and fold the egg in half to form an omelet.

Serve on a plate and spoon on the sweet chili sauce. Garnish with fresh parsley. Repeat with the remaining eggs.

> **TWEAK THE HEAT:** You are free to use whatever peppers you can handle with this recipe. I've made them with a huge range and, as expected, achieved a range of heat. I prefer bright, colorful peppers in the mid-range, which I've used here, such as jalapeños, serranos and red fingerlings. I've also made them with habaneros and 7-Pot peppers for some SERIOUS bang.

PREP
TIME

5 minutes

COOKING
TIME

30 minutes

SERVES

4-6

HEAT
LEVEL

Medium

Spicy Chili and
SPINACH FRITTATA

Frittatas are super easy to make. They're also a wonderful choice for clearing out your produce drawer. So, if you have extra mushrooms, peppers or other vegetables on hand, feel free to toss them into the mix. This version focuses on peppers for that spicy goodness we all crave.

1 tbsp (15 ml) olive oil

1½ cups (255 g) chopped spicy peppers (I used a mix of jalapeño, banana and cherry peppers)

8 oz (225 g) chopped spinach

6 oz (170 g) soppressata or spicy salami

12 eggs

½ cup (120 ml) heavy cream

1 cup (121 g) shredded cheddar cheese, divided

Salt and pepper to taste

Pinch of spicy chili flakes, plus more for serving

Fresh chopped parsley and your favorite hot sauce, for serving

Preheat the oven to 350°F (180°C).

Heat a large ovenproof pan to medium heat and add the oil with the spicy peppers. Cook them for about 5 minutes, until softened. Add the spinach and cook for another minute, until softened. Stir in the soppressata.

In a large bowl, beat the eggs and heavy cream together until the mixture is smooth. Stir in half of the cheese with a pinch of salt, pepper and spicy chili flakes. Pour the mixture into the pan and cook for about 5 minutes, or until the egg mixture starts to set.

Top the eggs with the remaining cheddar cheese and place the pan in the oven. Bake for 20 to 25 minutes, or until the center is set and the frittata is nicely browned.

Sprinkle with fresh parsley and extra chili flakes. Serve with your favorite hot sauce.

TWEAK THE HEAT: You can easily adjust the types and amounts of chili peppers used in this recipe, so if you're looking for a hotter version, introduce a habanero to the mix, or something even hotter. You can make a mild version by using bell peppers and going easy on the chili flakes.

Chiles Rellenos French Toast
WITH SPICED MAPLE SYRUP

PREP
TIME

10 minutes

COOKING
TIME

20 minutes

SERVES

4

HEAT
LEVEL

Mild-Medium

French toast was my mother's go-to breakfast when I was growing up. It was one of the first recipes I learned to make on my own. As I've grown older, I've come to appreciate more savory versions, though I still enjoy a touch of the sweet, which is how this recipe originated. It's a mashup of sorts; sweet from the infused maple syrup and savory from the classic flavors of Mexican chiles rellenos (stuffed peppers).

FOR THE STUFFING

2 medium-sized poblano peppers, sliced in half, lengthwise

8 oz (227 g) cream cheese, softened

1 tsp spicy chili flakes

Pinch of sea salt

FOR THE SYRUP

½ cup (120 ml) maple syrup

1 tsp spicy chili flakes

Pinch of sea salt

FOR THE FRENCH TOAST

2 tbsp (29 g) butter

4 eggs

½ cup (120 ml) milk

1 tbsp (15 ml) maple syrup

8 slices potato bread

Set the oven to broil.

Set the poblano peppers on a baking sheet, skin sides up. Broil them for 10 minutes, or until the skins have loosened and charred. Remove and cool them slightly, then peel off the skins. It helps to cover them with a paper towel to allow the skins to steam and loosen some more. Roughly chop the poblano peppers and add them to a large mixing bowl with the cream cheese, chili flakes and sea salt. Mix well.

In a small pan set to low heat, add the maple syrup, chili flakes and sea salt. Allow the syrup to steep with the pepper flakes, at least 5 minutes. Do not let the mixture boil. The goal is to infuse the syrup with the dried chili heat. You can strain out the flakes if you'd like, or leave them in like I do.

Heat a large pan to medium-high heat. Add the butter and let it melt over the pan. In a large bowl, beat together the eggs, milk and maple syrup. Dip the bread slices, one at a time, into the batter. Make sure each side is well-coated, but don't let the bread get soggy. Place the soaked bread slices on the hot pan and cook them for a couple minutes per side, until they are nicely browned. You'll need to do this in a couple batches.

For serving, set one slice of toast on a plate, then scoop about a quarter of the cream cheese mixture on it. Top with another slice of toast, then drizzle with the spicy syrup.

TWEAK THE HEAT: You can easily add a bit more heat by sprinkling a bit of spicy chili powder into your batter or over the bread as they toast in the buttered pan.

Slow & Spicy
(Slow Cooker Recipes)

Slow cookers make everything easy. So, often I'll just toss my ingredients in the pot and go about my business while an amazing meal practically makes itself. The majority of the work is in your prep work, a bit of chopping here and there, opening a can of this or that and lifting the lid of the slow cooker.

Easy is nice, isn't it? I love how the aromas from the slow cooker fill the house as I'm working, wafting out of the kitchen, like a big tease, begging me to lift the lid and take a taste.

The slow cooker is ideal for cooking tough cuts of meat that benefit from low and slow cooking, like certain selections of beef, though it's also perfect for making soups and stews. Also, the slow cooking process helps to accentuate your selection of spices, so if you love your meals with a bit of a kick, the slow cooker is certainly for you.

PREP
TIME

10 minutes

COOKING
TIME

15 minutes,
plus 6 to 8
hours in the
slow cooker

SERVES

4-6

HEAT
LEVEL

Medium

Slow-Cooked Corned Beef
WITH STOUT GRAVY

This might become your new favorite St. Patrick's Day recipe, though it's so good, I refuse to make it only once a year. When you cook corned beef on low heat, it becomes fork tender and practically melts in your mouth. The gravy made from the stout beer is rich, thick and very easy to make.

FOR THE CORNED BEEF
3 lb (1.3 kg) corned beef brisket
2 tbsp (30 ml) olive oil
3 jalapeño peppers, chopped
1 stalk celery, chopped
1 large onion, chopped
3 cloves garlic, chopped

FOR THE GRAVY
2 (12-oz [355-ml]) bottles stout beer
3–4 tbsp (48–64 g) spicy mustard
2 tbsp (40 g) honey
1 tbsp (14 g) butter
1 tbsp (8 g) all-purpose flour

Rinse the corned beef thoroughly to reduce the saltiness. If it comes with a seasoning packet, toss it out. Pat the corned beef brisket dry and set aside.

Heat a pan to medium heat and add the olive oil. Add the jalapeño peppers, celery and onion. Cook for about 5 minutes to soften, stirring occasionally.

Add the garlic and cook another minute.

In a separate bowl, combine the stout beer, mustard and honey.

Add the corned beef, beer-mustard mixture, jalapeños, celery and onions to the slow cooker.

Slow cook on low for 6 to 8 hours, until the brisket is very tender. You should be able to easily insert a fork into the meat. If it is not tender enough, leave it to cook longer. Set the beef on a plate.

For the gravy, strain out the liquids from the brisket into a separate bowl. Reserve about a cup (240 ml). Discard the vegetables.

Melt the butter in a pan over medium heat. Swirl in the flour and stir to form a roux. Cook for a couple of minutes to brown nicely. Add the strained juices from the corned beef and reduce the heat to a simmer. Stir often to thicken the gravy.

Slice the corned beef against the grain and drizzle with gravy. I like to serve mine with mashed potatoes.

TWEAK THE HEAT: You can easily add heat to this dish with other seasonings and hotter peppers, such as the habanero pepper, though you'll already get a high level of flavor from the corned beef and thick gravy.

Beer Brat Soup

I live just over the border of Wisconsin, so I've had my fair share of both beer and bratwurst. It is total beer and brat country here, reflected in this hearty stew. It's made with pale lager, seared bratwurst sausages and a medley of down-home vegetables with some spicy peppers for that extra kick. I use Wisconsin beer for this, but any good lager will do.

1 tbsp (15 ml) olive oil

5 bratwurst sausages

3 medium baking potatoes, chopped

1 large carrot, chopped

2 stalks celery, chopped

2 small red onions, chopped

1 red bell pepper, chopped

2 habanero peppers, chopped

8 oz (225 g) fresh baby spinach, chopped

2 (12-oz [355-ml]) bottles pale lager beer

1 tbsp (7 g) smoked paprika

1 tbsp (9 g) garlic powder

2 tbsp (32 g) spicy brown mustard

Salt and pepper to taste

2–3 tbsp (16–24 g) all-purpose flour, if desired

Shredded cheddar cheese, for serving

Heat a large pan to medium heat and add the olive oil. Add the brats and sear them for 5 minutes per side. Cool slightly. At this point, you can either add them directly to the slow cooker, or slice them first and add them to the slow cooker. Either way works great, though I prefer them sliced.

Add the potatoes, carrot, celery, onions, red bell pepper, habanero peppers, spinach, beer, paprika, garlic powder, mustard, salt and pepper to the slow cooker and stir. Cook on medium heat for 3 to 4 hours.

At about 3 hours, taste and adjust for salt and pepper. If you'd like a thicker stew, swirl the flour with some of the liquid from the stew until no lumps remain. Then, pour it into the stew and cook for another hour. Top with shredded cheese before serving.

TWEAK THE HEAT: If you'd like to tame the heat, cut back on the habaneros or omit them altogether. You can core out the innards for a bit less heat as well. Consider swapping in other peppers or, if you're like me, add in a couple more to REALLY up the heat!

PREP TIME

15 minutes

COOKING TIME

10 minutes, plus 4 hours in the slow cooker

SERVES

4

HEAT LEVEL

Hot–Very Hot

PREP
TIME

15 minutes

COOKING
TIME

20 minutes,
plus 6 hours
in the slow
cooker

SERVES

4

HEAT
LEVEL

Mild

Roasted Poblano—Tomatillo
CHILI WITH PORK

You haven't had chili until you've had this version. Tender pork loin, earthy roasted poblano peppers and tomatillos come together to create one of my favorite dishes. The only work here is in roasting the poblano peppers, which roast up quickly in the broiler. Then, it's "set it and forget it." Just dump it all into the slow cooker and go about your business until it's done.

4 large poblano peppers, sliced in half, lengthwise

2 tbsp (30 ml) olive oil

2 lb (907 g) pork loin roast, chopped

Salt and pepper to taste

2 jalapeño peppers, chopped

4 cloves garlic, chopped

2 lbs (907 g) tomatillos, husks removed, quartered

2 (15-oz [425-g]) cans cannelloni beans, drained

3 tbsp (27 g) chili powder

3 cups (720 ml) chicken broth

Chopped cilantro, crumbly white cheese, sliced limes, avocado and sliced jalapeños, for serving

Set the oven to broil. Place the poblano peppers on a baking dish, skin sides up. Broil them for 15 to 20 minutes, until the skins blacken and char. Remove them from the heat and let them cool enough to handle. Peel off the puffy skins and discard them. Roughly chop the poblanos and toss them into the slow cooker.

Heat a large pan to medium heat and add the olive oil. Season the pork with a pinch of salt and pepper. Add the pork and jalapeño peppers to the pan and cook them for about 5 minutes. You want a dark crust to start to form on the pork.

Add the garlic and cook another minute, stirring. Toss the whole thing into the slow cooker.

Add the tomatillos, cannelloni beans, chili powder, chicken broth, salt and pepper to the slow cooker. Cook for 6 hours on low. Scoop the chili into bowls and garnish with chopped cilantro, crumbly white cheese, sliced limes, avocado and sliced jalapeños.

HOT TIP: If you'd like a thinner consistency to your chili, add more stock to the mix. As a flavor enhancer, try using beer instead of broth. I like to use a strong IPA.

TWEAK THE HEAT: Poblano peppers are very low on the heat scale, though you'll get a HUGE amount of flavor with them, particularly from the roasting. If you're looking for more heat, toss in a few hotter peppers, or increase the amount of chili powder.

Slow Cooker Southwest
CHIPOTLE CHICKEN AND POBLANO STEW

Moving forward, this may become one of your go-to slow cooker recipes. It has a wonderful level of spiciness from the combination of seasonings and chipotles, plus you can easily make a larger batch for leftovers the next day. It's also very little effort for big results. The only work involved is chopping and waiting.

PREP TIME

15 minutes

COOKING TIME

4 hours in the slow cooker

SERVES

4-6

HEAT LEVEL

Medium

2 boneless chicken breasts, chopped

1 cup (211 g) rice (I used a long grain wheat rice)

2 large poblano peppers, chopped

1 jalapeño pepper, chopped

2 medium yellow onions, chopped

1 (15-oz [425-g]) can fire roasted tomatoes

1 (7-oz [198-g]) can chipotles in adobo sauce

1 (16-oz [453-g]) bag frozen corn

4 cups (960 ml) chicken broth

3 tbsp (45 g) of your favorite taco seasoning

1 tsp garlic powder

1 tsp cumin

Salt and pepper to taste

Fresh chopped cilantro, shredded cheese and hot sauce, for serving

In a large slow cooker, add the chicken, rice, poblano peppers, jalapeño, onions, tomatoes, chipotles, corn, chicken broth, taco seasoning, garlic powder, cumin, salt and pepper. Stir well. Cook on high for 4 hours. Give it another good stir.

Serve in bowls and top with fresh chopped cilantro, shredded cheese and a few drops of your favorite hot sauce, if desired.

TWEAK THE HEAT: This stew has quite a lot of zest factor, which might surprise you since the only heat elements are jalapeño, chipotles and a seasoning blend. You can easily increase the heat factor by adding hotter peppers or more seasonings. Omit the jalapeño and limit your seasonings for a milder version.

PREP
TIME

10 minutes

COOKING
TIME

10 minutes,
plus 4 to 5
hours in the
slow cooker

SERVES

4-6

HEAT
LEVEL

Hot

Spicy Slow Cooker
BUTTER CHICKEN

Butter chicken is an Indian dish that results in a fairly rich and creamy gravy that is almost buttery. It is incredibly easy to prepare, needing only a few minutes of chopping and pan cooking. After that, everything goes into a slow cooker. You only need to stir in a bit of optional cream at the end and cook some rice. My version goes heavy on the spices and really jacks things up for you.

1 tbsp (15 ml) olive oil
2 jalapeño peppers, chopped
1 serrano pepper, chopped
1 large onion, chopped
3 cloves garlic, chopped
1 (14-oz [414-ml]) can coconut milk
6 oz (170 g) tomato paste
2 lbs (907 g) skinless, boneless chicken thighs, chopped

2 tsp (4 g) garam masala
2 tsp (4 g) curry powder
1 tsp chili powder
1 tsp hot pepper flakes, plus extra for serving
1 tsp ginger powder
½ tsp turmeric
Salt and pepper to taste
Cooked rice and fresh chopped parsley, for serving

Heat a pan to medium heat and add the olive oil. Add the jalapeño peppers, serrano pepper and onion. Cook for about 5 minutes, stirring occasionally, until softened.

Add the garlic and cook for another minute.

Add the coconut milk and tomato paste. Stir well. Cook for another couple of minutes to let the sauce thicken.

Rub the chicken down with the garam masala, curry powder, chili powder, hot pepper flakes, ginger powder, turmeric and salt and pepper. Add it to the slow cooker and pour the sauce mixture over it. Slow cook on low for 4 to 5 hours. You can leave it in longer, if desired. Add a bit of water or chicken broth if needed to thin it out.

Serve over rice, and garnish with fresh chopped parsley and pepper flakes.

TWEAK THE HEAT: Serranos makes this a nice and spicy dish, though you can REALLY spice it up with some fresh ghost peppers or dried ghost pepper flakes. Indian cooking takes to ghost peppers quite nicely. Habanero peppers are great; they aren't as hot as ghost peppers, but they are hotter than serranos. If you'd prefer a milder version, skip the serrano peppers and dial back on the hot pepper flakes and seasoning blends. You'll still get plenty of flavor without all the heat.

Chunky Fire-Roasted
TOMATO-STUFFED
PEPPER SOUP

Stuffed peppers are an all-time favorite of mine, but when you make them into a soup, it takes them to the next level. What I love about this soup is that I am not limited to any single pepper, so I can make it as thick and fiery as I'd like, while focusing on the flavor. Fire roasted tomatoes are a MUST for this recipe, so be sure to seek them out at your local grocer.

PREP TIME

10 minutes

COOKING TIME

10 minutes, plus 3 to 4 hours in the slow cooker

SERVES

4

HEAT LEVEL

Medium-Hot

1 tbsp (15 ml) olive oil

1 medium onion, chopped

1 large sweet pepper, chopped

1 large Cubanelle pepper, chopped (or sub in a bell pepper)

1 serrano pepper, chopped

1 jalapeño pepper, chopped

4 cloves garlic, chopped

1 lb (454 g) ground turkey

1 tsp dried basil

1 tsp paprika

½ tsp cumin

Salt and pepper to taste

2 (14-oz [397-g]) cans fire roasted tomatoes

1 cup (240 ml) chicken broth

Fresh squeezed lime juice, fresh chopped parsley, chopped peppers and your favorite hot sauce, for serving

Heat a large pan to medium heat and add the olive oil. Add the onion, sweet pepper, Cubanelle pepper, serrano and jalapeño peppers. Cook them for about 5 minutes. Add the garlic, ground turkey, basil, paprika, cumin, salt and pepper. Break up the turkey into chunks with a wooden spoon, browning the outer edges. Cook for a minute or two, occasionally stirring.

In a slow cooker, add the turkey mixture, fire roasted tomatoes and chicken broth. Stir well.

Slow cook on low for 3 to 4 hours. Serve in bowls with a squeeze of fresh lime juice. Garnish with parsley, extra sliced peppers and your favorite hot sauce.

TWEAK THE HEAT: Serrano peppers always deliver a good level of heat, which might be just right for you, though it might get lost in the pot for those who love it HOT. Feel free to toss in another serrano, or go big with a habanero or two. If it's too hot for you, go with jalapeño peppers, or even skip the hot ones altogether. You'll still get big flavor.

PREP
TIME

10 minutes

COOKING
TIME

4 to 7 hours
in the slow
cooker

SERVES

8

HEAT
LEVEL

Medium

Spiced Lentil Soup with
SPANISH CHORIZO

My mother used to make split pea or lentil soup when I was growing up. It's a craving I've carried with me ever since. They're so incredibly easy to make—just toss everything into a slow cooker and wait until it's done. The only work is in chopping a few ingredients. Of course, I had to adapt the recipe from my mom's way of cooking. This is one of my favorite spicy versions.

2 jalapeño peppers, chopped

1 large sweet pepper, chopped

1 Fresno pepper, chopped

1 stalk celery, chopped

1 large onion, chopped

6 cloves garlic, chopped

2½ cups (565 g) chopped yellow potatoes

2 cups (402 g) lentils, rinsed

8 cups (1.9 L) chicken broth or vegetable broth

8 oz (227 g) Spanish chorizo, sliced

2 tbsp (30 g) Creole seasoning blend

1 tsp spicy chili flakes, plus more for serving

Salt and pepper to taste

1 cup (60 g) chopped parsley, plus more for serving

¼ cup (60 ml) red wine vinegar

Shredded Parmesan cheese, chili oil, lime juice and crusty bread, for serving

In the slow cooker, add the jalapeño peppers, sweet pepper, Fresno pepper, celery, onion, garlic, potatoes, lentils, chicken broth and Spanish chorizo. Next add the Creole seasoning, chili flakes, salt and pepper. Cover and cook on high for 4 to 5 hours, or on low for 6 to 7 hours.

Swirl in the parsley and red wine vinegar. Taste and adjust for salt and pepper.

Serve in bowls and top with Parmesan cheese, extra parsley, spicy chili flakes, chili oil, lime juice and some crusty bread.

HOT TIP: You can process some of the potatoes and lentils in a food processor, then return it to the pot if you'd like a creamier version. It depends on your desired consistency.

TWEAK THE HEAT: You'll get some great flavor and a nice kick from the Spanish chorizo, chili peppers and Creole seasoning. But, if you're looking to dial back on the heat, omit the spicier peppers and go with milder ones. To bump up the heat, find a spicier Creole blend or incorporate hotter peppers.

Power Under Pressure

I love my pressure cooker. I used to cook with an older stovetop model my mother-in-law gave me because she didn't use it anymore. I currently use an electric model, though the more popular version is the Instant Pot. It doesn't matter which type you use, as long as it achieves the same goal—cooking foods in a fraction of the time it takes with more traditional methods.

With a pressure cooker, you can cook tough cuts of meat so much faster. Consider this—tender pork ribs in 45 minutes, pulled pork in 80 minutes and oxtail stew in under an hour. These types of meals normally take hours and hours to cook in a slow cooker. With a pressure cooker, you will save a lot of time.

These are some easy recipes with big, bold flavors that only a pressure cooker can deliver.

PREP
TIME

10 minutes

COOKING
TIME

4 minutes

SERVES

6-8

HEAT
LEVEL

Medium

Creole-Style
MAC AND CHEESE

Four minutes of cooking is all you need with this Creole version of your favorite mac and cheese. I use plenty of seasoning, hot sauce, pepper Jack cheese and smoked ham to give it a nice spin.

1 lb (454 g) uncooked pasta noodles (I used medium shells)

4 cups (960 ml) water or chicken broth

10 oz (283 g) smoked ham, cubed

3 tbsp (45 ml) Louisiana-style hot sauce, plus more for serving

2 jalapeño peppers, chopped, plus more for serving

4 tbsp (57 g) butter

2 tbsp (30 g) Creole seasoning blend

1 tsp salt

¾ cup (180 ml) 2% milk

2-3 cups (260-390 g) shredded pepper Jack cheese

In a pressure cooker, add the pasta noodles, water, smoked ham, hot sauce, jalapeños, butter, Creole seasoning and salt. Stir well.

Secure the lid and pressure cook on high for 4 minutes. When the timer goes off, release the steam, then remove the lid. Stir in the milk and cheese, until the cheese is melted through.

Serve with extra hot sauce and top with chopped jalapeño peppers.

HOT TIPS: You will have a richer flavor if you use chicken broth with this recipe, though water works just as well.

Two cups of cheese (260 g) will make this nice and cheesy, but the pot can easily absorb more cheese, so if you're seeking an extra cheesy dish, add an extra cup (130 g) of cheese. Also, feel free to change up the choice of cheese. Cheddar is always a great option.

You can easily buy smoked ham from your grocer, but this recipe also works nicely with leftover smoked ham for those who, like myself, enjoy smoking their own meats.

TWEAK THE HEAT: For extra heat, add more hot sauce.

Baby Back Ribs with
SAMBAL BBQ SAUCE

It usually takes many hours of low and slow cooking to make ribs at home, but with a pressure cooker, you can have them in under an hour. These are fall-off-the-bone tender and made extra flavorful with a quick and easy, and slightly spicy, BBQ sauce.

You can also pressure cook more than one rack at a time. I shared this exact recipe with a buddy of mine and he made 3 at once.

FOR THE RIBS
1 rack of baby back ribs
3 tbsp (22 g) smoked paprika
1 tbsp (7 g) cayenne powder
1 tbsp (9 g) garlic powder
2 tbsp (18 g) onion powder
Salt and pepper to taste
½ cup (120 ml) apple cider vinegar
¼ cup (60 ml) water

FOR THE SAUCE
½ cup (122 g) sambal oelek
3 tbsp (45 ml) soy sauce
2 tbsp (30 ml) Worcestershire sauce
1 tbsp (7 g) cayenne powder
Salt to taste

Remove the membrane from the back of the ribs. Combine the paprika, cayenne, garlic and onion powder, salt and pepper. Thoroughly rub the ribs down with the seasoning mix. Set the ribs into the pressure cooker, wrapping it around the pot, meat side outward. You can also quarter the ribs and set them bone side down inside the pot.

Add the apple cider vinegar and water, and secure the lid. Pressure cook on high for 30 minutes. Let the pressure release naturally, about 10 to 15 minutes.

While the ribs are cooking, combine the sambal oelek, soy sauce, Worcestershire, cayenne and salt in a saucepan on medium-low heat. Stir and cook for 10 minutes.

Brush the sauce over the ribs. Slice before serving.

HOT TIP: Be sure to follow your specific pressure cooker guidelines for liquid levels and operation.

TWEAK THE HEAT: For extra heat factor, go heavy on the cayenne powder, which has a nice kick to it. Sambal oelek is a chili paste similar to sriracha, though not nearly as sweet as the American version. Feel free to substitute with sriracha, or add some in for extra sweet heat.

PREP TIME

10 minutes

COOKING TIME

45 minutes

MAKES

1 rack of ribs

HEAT LEVEL

Medium

PREP
TIME

10 minutes

COOKING
TIME

1 hour and 20
minutes

SERVES

12

HEAT
LEVEL

Medium

Sweet and Spicy
PULLED PORK

Pork shoulder is a tougher cut of meat that requires long, slow cooking to make tender. With a pressure cooker, it only takes an hour or so. There is very little cooking involved, and the result is pork that is so tender, it literally comes apart with your fingers. I often make a 5-pound (2.3-kg) shoulder and use it all week for sandwiches, tacos, skillets and more.

1 (5-lb [2.3-kg]) pork shoulder, bone-in

3 tbsp (45 ml) olive oil, divided

3 tbsp (45 g) brown sugar

3 tbsp (22 g) paprika

2 tbsp (14 g) cayenne powder

2 tbsp (18 g) garlic powder

2 tbsp (18 g) onion powder

1 tsp cumin

Salt and pepper to taste

16 oz (475 ml) of your favorite lager

Cut the pork shoulder into large cubes. Be sure to cut around the bone. Rub the meat down with 2 tablespoons (30 ml) of olive oil. Combine the brown sugar, paprika, cayenne, garlic and onion powder, cumin, salt and pepper, and rub it thoroughly into the meat.

In a hot pan, sear the meat in the remaining tablespoon (15 ml) of the olive oil, about 2 to 3 minutes per side and until nicely browned.

Set the meat and beer into the pressure cooker and seal. Cook on high pressure for 60 minutes, then release the pressure naturally for about 10 to 15 minutes.

Remove the bone and place the meat in a large bowl. Shred with forks.

Serve on sandwich rolls with melty cheese, over tortillas with plenty of taco fixings, with your favorite barbecue sauce, over rice or however you'd like to enjoy it. Store the leftovers in a sealable container in the fridge for a week, or freeze it for up to 6 months.

HOT TIP: Feel free to substitute the beer with other liquids for flavor variations. Chicken or beef broth is a tasty alternative.

TWEAK THE HEAT: You'll get a good spice level from the generous use of seasonings, though plenty of sweetness from the brown sugar. If you'd like to increase the heat factor, look for spicier rubs or blends, such as ghost pepper powder. You can also toss in a few chopped chili peppers into the pressure cooker—they will permeate the meat.

NOTE: Five pounds (2.3 kg) of pork shoulder yields about 3 pounds (1.4 kg) of cooked meat. Your serving size may vary, depending on your recipe.

PREP
TIME

5 minutes

COOKING
TIME

5 minutes, plus
30 minutes in
the pressure
cooker

SERVES

6–8

HEAT
LEVEL

Medium

Country-Style Pork Ribs
WITH SWEET AND SPICY CRANBERRY SAUCE

Country style pork ribs are quite different from baby back ribs. They are cut from the blade end, close to the pork shoulder, and are typically meatier than other cuts. The flavor is closer to that of pork shoulder, and they become very tender in the pressure cooker. The sauce is meaty and slightly tart from the cranberry and orange combination, with a nice level of spiciness.

FOR THE RIBS
3½–4 lb (1.6–1.8 kg) country-style pork ribs
2 tbsp (30 ml) olive oil
1 tbsp (9 g) chili powder
1 tsp garlic powder
1 tsp onion powder
Salt and pepper to taste

FOR THE SAUCE
1 (14-oz [397-g]) can cranberry sauce
1 cup (240 ml) orange juice
1 serrano pepper, chopped
1 small onion, chopped
1 cup (240 ml) sriracha
1 tbsp (15 ml) Worcestershire sauce
⅓ cup (67 g) brown sugar
1 tbsp (8 g) spicy chili flakes
1 tbsp (8 g) flour or cornstarch, if desired

Set your pressure cooker to "browning." Rub the ribs down with olive oil, then sprinkle them with the chili powder, garlic and onion powder and a pinch of salt and pepper. Sear the ribs for a couple minutes per side to get a nice crust on them. Alternatively, do this on a pan on the stovetop.

Add the cranberry sauce, orange juice, serrano pepper, onion, sriracha, Worcestershire, brown sugar and chili flakes to the pressure cooker. Secure the lid and pressure cook the ribs on high for 20 minutes. Allow the pressure to release naturally for about 10 minutes.

Remove the ribs and serve with some of the sauce from the cooker. If you'd like to thicken up the sauce, swirl together a tablespoon (8 g) of flour or cornstarch in water. Add it to the sauce and stir while warming.

Serve with a quick, spicy potato mash, if desired.

*See photo on page 124.

TWEAK THE HEAT: The chili flakes and, particularly, the serrano pepper will permeate the sauce for a good level of spiciness. If you're looking for more heat, toss in extra serranos and chili flakes, or go with a hotter pepper, such as a Scotch bonnet or habanero.

QUICK SPICY POTATO MASH

I love to serve these pork ribs over mashed potatoes when I'm craving comfort food. The key to making these quickly is to use the "potato" setting on your microwave. Of course, you can still make these in the oven if you don't own a microwave. Just bake them until they are cooked through. However, the microwave is a heck of a time saver.

2 lbs (930 g) potatoes

2 tbsp (29 g) butter

2 tbsp (30 g) Mexican crema or sour cream

1 tbsp (12 g) Cajun seasoning blend

1 tsp garlic powder

1 tsp sriracha

Poke the potatoes with a fork. Microwave the potatoes on the "potato" setting, or for about 10 minutes, until they are cooked and softened all the way through. You'll know they are done when an inserted knife goes through.

In a bowl, mash the potatoes, butter, crema, Cajun seasoning, garlic powder and sriracha. A large fork works great for this.

PREP TIME

5 minutes

COOKING TIME

15 minutes

SERVES

6–8

HEAT LEVEL

Mild-Medium

Spicy Caribbean OXTAIL STEW

Long ago, oxtail was, literally, the tail of the ox, but today it comes from cow tails. It is a very tough cut of meat that usually requires long, slow cooking on low heat. With a pressure cooker, you can accomplish in 40 minutes what would take 3 plus hours in a slow cooker. The result is beef that will melt in your mouth. This recipe brings in flavors from the Caribbean.

PREP TIME

5 minutes

COOKING TIME

55 minutes

SERVES

4

HEAT LEVEL

Medium-Hot

3 lb (1.4 kg) oxtail
1 tbsp (7 g) cayenne powder
1 tbsp (7 g) paprika
1 tsp garlic powder
1 tsp allspice
½ tsp nutmeg
Salt and pepper to taste
2 tbsp (30 ml) olive oil, divided
3 Scotch bonnet peppers, chopped
1 cup (175 g) chopped sweet peppers

1 small white onion, chopped
3 garlic cloves, chopped
1 tsp spicy red pepper flakes
1 tbsp (7 g) butter
2 tbsp (16 g) all-purpose flour
6 oz (170 g) tomato paste
4 cups (960 ml) beef broth (or chicken or vegetable stock)
Cooked rice or pasta noodles, for serving

Season the oxtail liberally with the cayenne, paprika, garlic powder, allspice, nutmeg, salt and pepper.

In a large pan, heat a tablespoon (15 ml) of the olive oil and sear the oxtail a few minutes per side, until browned. You can use your pressure cooker for this on the "sauté" setting, but I find it easier to use a large pan. Transfer the oxtail to the pressure cooker.

In the same pan, add the remaining olive oil and cook the Scotch bonnet peppers, sweet peppers and onion for about 4 minutes, to soften. Add the garlic and cook until fragrant. Add the red pepper flakes, butter and flour. Stir until the butter is melted and cook for about 3 minutes to thicken.

Add the tomato paste and about a ¼ cup (60 ml) of water. Cook for a couple minutes, stirring, until everything is nicely incorporated. Pour the contents into the pressure cooker along with the stock.

Pressure cook the oxtail on high pressure for 40 minutes. Release the pressure naturally.

Break the meat apart and remove the bones. Discard them and add the meat back to the pot. The liquid will be somewhat thin.

Serve the oxtail over cooked rice or noodles, then ladle a bit of the seasoned cooking liquid over the top.

HOT TIP: I like to keep the sauce thin to lightly coat the oxtail when serving, but if you'd like, you can thicken up the sauce by swirling a few tablespoons of flour or cornstarch in equal amounts water until no lumps remain, then stir it into the sauce. Let it simmer until the sauce thickens up.

PREP
TIME

15 minutes

COOKING
TIME

15 minutes

SERVES

4

HEAT
LEVEL

Medium-Hot

Huli Huli Chicken
TACOS WITH PINEAPPLE-SERRANO SALSA

Enjoy the wonderful combination of sweet and spicy with this recipe for chicken with pineapple-serrano salsa. Your pressure cooker makes the meal a snap. The chicken shreds up easily and soaks up the sauce.

1 tsp olive oil

1 small onion, chopped

2 serrano peppers, chopped, plus more for serving

1½ lbs (681 g) chicken breast, chopped

1 cup (165 g) chopped pineapple, plus more for serving

¼ cup (60 ml) sriracha

¼ cup (60 g) brown sugar

¼ cup (60 ml) pineapple juice

1 tbsp (7 g) cayenne powder

1 tsp garlic powder

1 tsp ground ginger

Salt and pepper to taste

Warmed tortillas, fresh chopped cilantro, lime wedges and hot sauce, for serving

Set the pressure cooker to "sauté." Add the olive oil, onion and serrano peppers. Cook them down for about 5 minutes to soften.

Add the chicken, pineapple, sriracha, brown sugar, pineapple juice, cayenne, garlic powder, ginger, salt and pepper. Pressure cook on high for 10 minutes, then release the pressure naturally.

Shred the chicken in the sauce with a couple of forks. It should pull apart very easily.

Serve on warmed tortillas topped with extra serrano peppers, pineapple, fresh chopped cilantro, lime wedges and hot sauce.

TWEAK THE HEAT: Serrano peppers pack a decent amount of heat. If you're looking for a milder version of this recipe, use jalapeño peppers instead. If you're looking to increase the heat factor, include more serrano peppers or introduce some hotter peppers, such as habaneros, Scotch bonnets or even ghost peppers. Bring on the heat!

Easy Risotto with
HOT ITALIAN SAUSAGE

I've made risotto dozens of times in my life. It is one of my favorite dishes and the pressure cooker makes it super easy. This is the fastest way to make risotto; it takes little effort, and it's just as tasty. I enjoy adding a mixture of different peppers and meats for a heartier dish.

1 tbsp (15 ml) olive oil

1 shallot, chopped

1 sweet Italian pepper, chopped (or red bell pepper)

1 serrano pepper, chopped, plus more for serving

1 lb (454 g) hot Italian sausage, chopped

2 cloves garlic, chopped

1 cup (211 g) Arborio rice

½ cup (120 ml) white wine

2½ cups (595 ml) chicken or vegetable stock

1 tsp salt

2 tbsp (30 ml) of your favorite hot sauce (I used a roasted garlic red pepper sauce)

Cracked black pepper, fresh chopped basil, grated Parmesan cheese and spicy chili flakes, for serving

Set your pressure cooker to the "sauté" setting. Add the olive oil, shallot, sweet pepper, serrano pepper and Italian sausage. Cook for about 3 to 4 minutes, stirring occasionally. Add the garlic; cook until fragrant.

Add the rice and cook for 2 minutes, stirring, then add the wine. Stir and let it cook until the wine incorporates, about 2 minutes or so. Add the stock, salt and hot sauce. Stir well. Set the pressure cooker to "low pressure" and cook for 8 minutes. When the time is up, release the pressure and open. Stir until creamy. If there is too much liquid, you can pressure cook it again for 2 to 3 more minutes.

Serve in bowls and top with cracked black pepper, fresh basil, grated Parmesan cheese, chili flakes and some pan-seared serrano peppers.

> TWEAK THE HEAT: I like to serve mine with quickly seared serrano peppers for additional heat. Simply heat a teaspoon of olive oil in a pan and add sliced serrano peppers. Cook them a couple minutes per side, until they've crisped to your liking. They add a good level of heat, though you can easily omit them for a milder version. You'll get plenty of flavor from the initial peppers and hot sauce.

PREP TIME

5 minutes

COOKING TIME

15 minutes

SERVES

4

HEAT LEVEL

Medium-Hot

PREP
TIME

10 minutes

COOKING
TIME

9 minutes,
plus 5 to 10
minutes in
the broiler, if
desired

SERVES

4

HEAT
LEVEL

Medium

Chicken Wings with
HOMEMADE BUFFALO SAUCE

With a pressure cooker, you can have super tender chicken wings done in 9 minutes. I like to pop them in the broiler to crisp them up a bit after cooking, but the choice is yours. I'm serving these with a traditional Buffalo sauce that is easier to prepare than you think. These wings are fall-off-the-bone delicious.

FOR THE CHICKEN WINGS

3 lbs (1.4 kg) chicken wings, separated, wing tips removed
2 tbsp (30 ml) olive oil
1 tbsp (7 g) paprika
1 tbsp (8 g) hot chili flakes
1 tbsp (9 g) garlic powder
Salt and pepper to taste
½ cup (120 ml) chicken broth or water

FOR THE BUFFALO SAUCE

1 stick butter
½ cup (120 ml) Louisiana-style hot sauce (such as Franks or Valentina)
2 tbsp (30 ml) apple cider vinegar
1 tsp Worcestershire sauce
1 tsp Tabasco sauce
1 tsp paprika
½ tsp garlic powder
Salt and pepper to taste

Rinse the wings and pat them dry. In a large mixing bowl, toss the wings with the olive oil, paprika, chili flakes, garlic powder, salt and pepper. Make sure to coat them evenly.

Add the wings and the chicken broth to the pressure cooker. Set the pressure to high and cook for 9 minutes.

Release the steam and carefully remove the wings. You can eat as is or for a crispier version, set them on a lightly-oiled baking sheet and broil for 5 minutes on each side.

To make the Buffalo sauce, melt the butter in a small pot. Whisk in the hot sauce, apple cider vinegar, Worcestershire, Tabasco, paprika, garlic powder, salt and pepper.

Toss the wings with the homemade Buffalo sauce.

HOT TIP: The Buffalo sauce can be considered a base recipe. Add in Parmesan cheese for a Buffalo-parmesan version. Mix in chopped jalapeño peppers and cheddar cheese for a jalapeño-cheddar version. Happy experimenting!

TWEAK THE HEAT: Buffalo sauce delivers a nice tang to the wings, though you won't get a ton of heat, just big flavor. I like to introduce extra spicy chili flakes, particularly dried ghost pepper flakes, into the seasoning for a hotter version.

Fired-Up Foods from Around the World

Spicy foods are enjoyed all over the world, and as a chili pepper fanatic, I enjoy following the peppers into other cuisines. Of course, we love them here in the U.S., but you'll find them practically everywhere in the world.

When I began to approach this chapter, I quickly became overwhelmed, because one could fill a thousand books with stories of spicy foods and recipes from around the world. So, I took a step back and decided to include some of my very favorites, of which there are many.

Many of these recipes are not authentic versions of those original cultural dishes, but rather filtered through my spicy cooking preferences. They are also perhaps a bit Americanized by the ingredients we have on hand here, but this is one of the beauties of cooking—its ultimate adaptability. This creative adaptability is how we've been gifted with gumbo, one of the best foods in the world, so of course, I'm including a gumbo recipe for you.

PREP
TIME

15 minutes

COOKING
TIME

60 to 70
minutes

SERVES

6

HEAT
LEVEL

Medium

Cajun Chicken and
SAUSAGE GUMBO

I'm starting this "Fired-Up Foods from Around the World" chapter with a very famous U.S. recipe—gumbo. The truth is, while gumbo may be a product of Louisiana, it owes its origins to a range of diverse cultures, including French, Spanish, African, Irish, American Indian, Italian, southern and more. In fact, gumbo is the official state cuisine of Louisiana. It is definitely one of my favorite foods and I simply had to include it.

Once you've learned how to make a good gumbo, you will love it for life. It may seem like a bit of work at first, but you only need to master the roux, which is quite easy. Everything else falls into its own delicious place. This is a classic Cajun version with chicken and smoked andouille sausage, though you can also add shrimp, crab, crawfish or even gator. When I learned to make gumbo from several chefs in New Orleans, I asked about their preferred seasonings and ingredients, and the invariable response was, "Whatever your momma taught you." If New Orleans chefs are allowed to be flexible, you can be too. This is my spicier version.

1 tsp olive oil

1 lb (454 g) chicken breast or thighs, roughly chopped

Salt and pepper to taste

12 oz (340 g) andouille sausage, sliced into ¼" (0.6-cm) slices

½ cup (120 ml) peanut oil or vegetable oil

½ cup (62 g) all-purpose flour

1 medium bell pepper, chopped

1–2 serrano peppers, chopped

1 medium onion, chopped

1 medium celery stalk, chopped

3 cloves garlic, chopped

2 tbsp (24 g) Cajun seasoning

1 tsp cayenne pepper

6 cups (1.4 L) chicken stock

3 bay leaves

1 tsp thyme

4 tbsp (15 g) chopped parsley, plus more for serving

1 tbsp (7 g) filé powder

Cooked white rice, for serving

In a large pot set to medium heat, add the olive oil and heat it through. Season the chicken with salt and pepper, and add to the pan with the sliced andouille. Cook for a couple minutes on each side, until everything is nicely browned. Set aside until ready to use.

Add the peanut oil to the pot and heat it to medium heat. Add the flour and stir. Cook for 15 to 20 minutes, constantly stirring, until the roux browns to the color of chocolate. The roux will begin to darken in stages as you stir, from a light brown to the color of peanut butter, to a light chocolate brown, then finally to a rich dark chocolate color. Some people prefer to stop cooking when the roux is the color of peanut butter, or perhaps a copper penny. Your gumbo will turn out a bit thicker this way, though it will still have plenty of flavor. Feel free to try it different ways to learn your own personal preference.

Do not allow your roux to burn. Use the bottom of a wooden spatula to constantly stir the roux around the pot. Keep it from sticking to the bottom, where it will burn. If you burn the roux, you'll smell it and need to start over.

(continued)

CAJUN CHICKEN AND SAUSAGE GUMBO (CONTINUED)

Once the roux has browned to your liking (I usually go for the color of peanut butter or light chocolate), add the bell pepper, serrano peppers, onion, celery and garlic. Stir and cook for about 5 minutes.

Add the cooked chicken and andouille. Stir and cook for a minute.

Add the Cajun seasoning, cayenne pepper and chicken stock. Scrape up the brown bits from the bottom of the pot. Add the bay leaves and thyme, and cook at medium-low heat for an hour to thicken, stirring occasionally.

Stir in the parsley and cook for 5 minutes to let it permeate.

Turn off the heat and stir in the filé powder. This will thicken it up a bit. Alternatively, you can stir the filé powder into each bowl, or use okra early on, though I prefer the powder.

Serve your gumbo over white rice and garnish with extra parsley.

HOT TIP: While okra was more traditional for gumbo back in the day, you'll find many Cajun and Creole chefs today opt for the filé powder, which is dried, ground sassafras leaves, in order to thicken their gumbos. Feel free to use either one, though if you'll be using okra, add it in earlier when you add the other vegetables.

TWEAK THE HEAT: Cajun food isn't known for its heat. Rather, it is known for its deep, intense flavors and generous use of seasonings. The story is that the Cajuns lived off whatever lived in their swampy lands and needed heavy seasonings to cover up the gamey taste. Luckily for us, the use of seasonings became a tradition. You can easily introduce hotter elements, such as spicy peppers or powders, though I don't think you'll need it with these flavors.

Spicy Asian Garlic Pasta

Because the sauce is basically a "no cook" sauce, you can have this recipe on the table in under 20 minutes. Most of the work is in chopping peppers. I like to use small, briny bay scallops, though feel free to use shrimp instead. Don't forget to pile on those peppers!

PREP
TIME

10 minutes

COOKING
TIME

20 minutes

SERVES

4

HEAT
LEVEL

Medium-Hot

FOR THE SAUCE
⅓ cup (80 ml) soy sauce
2 tbsp (30 g) brown sugar
1 tbsp (14 g) chili-garlic sauce
1 tbsp (15 ml) fish sauce
1 tsp dried ginger
1 tsp sesame oil
2 cloves garlic, minced

FOR THE PASTA
8 oz (227 g) spaghetti noodles (any thin noodle will do)
2 tbsp (30 ml) hot chili oil
1 large red sweet pepper, sliced into strips
1 large green sweet pepper, sliced into strips
3-4 Chinese hot peppers, chopped (or substitute with cayenne or serranos)
1 medium-sized carrot, peeled and grated
1 tsp hot chili flakes, plus more for serving
1 lb (454 g) bay scallops
10 fresh basil leaves, chopped
Chopped green onion, for serving

In a small bowl, combine the soy sauce, brown sugar, chili-garlic sauce, fish sauce, ginger, sesame oil and garlic. Set aside.

To make the spaghetti, bring a pot of salted water to a boil and add the spaghetti noodles. Cook them until al dente, about 10 minutes. Drain.

Heat a large wok or pan to medium-high heat. Add the chili oil, red pepper, green pepper and Chinese hot peppers. Cook them for about 5 minutes to soften. Add the carrot and chili flakes. Cook for a minute or so, stirring.

Add the scallops and sauce. Stir and cook for a couple minutes, or until all of the scallops are cooked through.

Remove the pan from the heat and stir in the fresh basil and drained pasta noodles. Toss well.

Serve in bowls and garnish with green onion and extra chili flakes.

*See photo on page 142.

TWEAK THE HEAT: Chinese peppers may be difficult to find if you don't have an ethnic market nearby, so feel free to substitute for spicier local peppers, such as serrano peppers or cayenne. Most of the pepper substance will be from the sweeter peppers, so feel free to experiment with the spicier peppers.

For the chili flakes, dried Sichuan chilies are great. However, Thai chilies or cayenne are an excellent substitute.

Bulgogi—
KOREAN BBQ BOWLS

The word "bulgogi" is a Korean word that translates to "fire meat," and WOW is it good. At its core, it is marinated meat, typically beef or pork, which is quickly cooked in a wok or pan over high heat. Because the meat is thinly sliced, it cooks fast, making for a quick and easy dinner option. I like to serve it in a few different ways, particularly with tortillas and toppings for Korean BBQ Tacos, or over rice with loads of fixings. I make mine spicier than most.

PREP TIME

15 minutes

COOKING TIME

15 minutes

SERVES

4

HEAT LEVEL

Medium–Hot

4 tbsp (60 ml) soy sauce
2 tbsp (30 g) gochujang
2 tbsp (30 ml) rice wine vinegar
2 tbsp (30 ml) sesame oil, divided
1 tbsp (20 g) honey
1 tsp ginger powder
1 spicy red fingerling pepper, minced
2 cloves garlic, minced
1 tbsp (8 g) hot pepper flakes, plus more for serving

Pinch of black pepper, plus more for serving
1½ lb (681 g) rib eye steak, sliced thinly or cubed
1 bunch asparagus tips, about 2 cups (250 g)
4 spicy red fingerling peppers, sliced
4 eggs
3 cups (483 g) prepared rice
Shredded carrot, sliced green onion and sesame seeds, for serving

In a small bowl, combine the soy sauce, gochujang, rice wine vinegar, a tablespoon (15 ml) of sesame oil, honey, ginger powder, red fingerling pepper, garlic, hot pepper flakes and a pinch of black pepper. Pour it into a large bowl with the sliced or cubed rib eye steak, asparagus tips and red fingerling peppers. Toss with a spoon. Cover and marinade for at least 5 minutes. If you have time, marinade it in the fridge for an hour or longer.

In a small pot, add water and salt and bring to a boil. Add the eggs and boil them for 6 minutes, then drain and submerge them into cold water. When they are cool enough to handle, gently peel them and set them aside.

In a wok or large pan set to medium-high heat, add the remaining sesame oil. Add the steak mixture (including the marinade) and cook, stirring often, for about 5 to 6 minutes, or until it is done to your liking.

Before serving, cut the eggs in half, being careful not to lose the drippy yolks.

Serve the rice in 4 bowls and top with the meat, egg, carrot, green onion, sesame seeds, cracked black pepper and extra hot pepper flakes.

TWEAK THE HEAT: Most of the heat factor in this recipe comes from your choice of peppers and chili flakes. If you have a hard time finding fingerling peppers, look for cayenne or serrano peppers. Jalapeño peppers work great for a lower level of heat. I've made my marinade with ghost peppers and it turns out great. For a milder version, omit the hot pepper flakes and use a red bell pepper. You will still achieve plenty of flavor.

PREP
TIME

10 minutes

COOKING
TIME

10 minutes

SERVES

4

HEAT
LEVEL

Medium-Hot

Thai Chicken and Noodles in
SPICY PEANUT SAUCE

Thai food is well known for the spiciness of some of its dishes, so naturally I gravitate toward it. This particular dish has a bit of heat, though it certainly delivers on flavor. It's also super easy to make. You'll have your meal on the table in well under 30 minutes.

3 tbsp (45 ml) sesame oil, divided

1 lb (454 g) chicken breast, chopped

1 large carrot, finely chopped

3-4 Thai chili peppers (or substitute with cayenne or serrano), plus more for garnish

3 cloves garlic, chopped

1 tbsp (14 g) Thai chili paste

¼ cup (45 g) creamy peanut butter

¼ cup (60 ml) soy sauce

3 tbsp (45 ml) rice wine vinegar

2 tbsp (28 g) chili-garlic sauce

8 oz (227 g) prepared Thai rice noodles

Crumbled spicy peanuts and fresh parsley, for serving

Heat a wok or large pan to medium heat and add a tablespoon (15 ml) of the sesame oil. Add the chicken, carrot and Thai chili peppers and cook them down, stirring occasionally, for about 8 minutes, or until the chicken is cooked through.

Add the garlic and Thai chili paste and stir. Cook for a minute, stirring.

Add the peanut butter, soy sauce, rice wine vinegar and chili-garlic sauce. Stir to incorporate. If the sauce is too thick, add in a couple splashes of water to bring it to your desired consistency.

In a pot, prepare the Thai rice noodles according to the packaging instructions, boiling for about 8 to 10 minutes in hot water. Drain, then toss the noodles with 2 tablespoons (30 ml) of the sesame oil.

Toss the noodles in the sauce. Serve in bowls and top with extra Thai chilies, spicy peanuts and fresh parsley.

TWEAK THE HEAT: Thai peppers can run pretty hot, ranging from 50,000 to 100,000 Scoville Heat Units (SHU). To compare, a jalapeño averages about 5,000 SHU. For additional heat, include more Thai peppers. If you have trouble finding Thai peppers, you can easily swap in cayenne peppers, or consider serranos, which are typically easier to find. Jalapeños are always an ideal go-to as well.

Pan-Seared Scallops over
HOT CHILI COUSCOUS
WITH HARISSA

PREP TIME

10 minutes

COOKING TIME

15 minutes

SERVES

4

HEAT LEVEL

Medium

Harissa is a spicy chili paste that is prominent in North African and Middle Eastern cooking. Recipes vary, but it typically includes hot peppers, garlic and a number of seasonings in oil. Chili pastes and sauces are a must in any spicy food lover's kitchen, particularly harissa for its flavor and versatility. It's perfect for this recipe, which you can have on the table in under 30 minutes.

FOR THE COUSCOUS

1 tbsp (15 ml) olive oil

1 shallot, chopped

1 medium poblano pepper, chopped

1 jalapeño pepper, chopped

2 cloves garlic, chopped

1 cup (173 g) couscous

1½ cups (360 ml) chicken or vegetable stock (water is fine)

1 tsp salt

1 tbsp (14 g) harissa, plus more for serving

FOR THE SCALLOPS

3 tbsp (43 g) butter

1 lb (454 g) sea scallops, thawed if frozen

1 tsp spicy chili powder

1 tsp garlic powder

Salt and pepper to taste

1 tbsp (14 g) harissa

Fresh chopped parsley and spicy chili flakes, for serving

In a medium pot, heat the olive oil, shallot, poblano and jalapeño pepper. Cook for about 4 to 5 minutes, stirring occasionally. Add the garlic and stir; cook until fragrant.

Add the couscous, stock and salt. Bring to a quick boil, then remove the pot from the heat. Stir in a tablespoon (14 g) of harissa and cover it. Allow the couscous to absorb the liquid, about 5 minutes.

In a large pan over medium-high heat, melt the butter. Pat dry and season the scallops with the chili and garlic powders, salt and pepper. Sear them in the pan for 2 minutes on each side. Remove from the heat and stir in a tablespoon (14 g) of harissa.

Fluff the couscous and serve it on plates. Top with the seared scallops, a few drizzles of extra harissa, if desired, some fresh parsley and chili flakes.

TWEAK THE HEAT: Harissa will give you a bit of a kick in the spice department, so adjust the amount you use depending on your preferred spice and heat level. I've used a jalapeño pepper for this recipe, but feel free to incorporate hotter peppers to kick it up a notch.

PREP
TIME

10 minutes

COOKING
TIME

20 minutes

SERVES

4

HEAT
LEVEL

Medium-Hot

Indian Chicken and
SWEET POTATO CURRY

There are SO many types of curry spices and blends in the world, so when it comes to curry, you can enjoy numerous variations and they are all delicious. I always look for curry seasonings with a bit of a kick, though it's easy to add in your own.

1 tbsp (15 ml) olive oil

1½ lbs (681 g) chicken breasts, chopped

Salt and pepper to taste

2 medium sweet potatoes, peeled and diced

1 small onion, chopped

1 cayenne pepper, chopped (or substitute with Thai or serrano)

1 tbsp (14 g) fresh chopped ginger

3 cloves garlic, chopped

1 tsp curry powder

1 tsp hot paprika

1 tsp cumin

1 tsp hot chili flakes, plus more for serving

1 cup (240 ml) chicken broth

1 (14-oz [397-g]) can chopped tomatoes

¼ cup (4 g) chopped cilantro, plus more for serving

Cooked rice, for serving

In a large pan set to medium heat, add the olive oil. Season the chicken breasts with salt and pepper. Add them to the pan with the sweet potatoes, onion, cayenne pepper and ginger. Cook for 5 minutes, stirring occasionally.

Add the garlic and cook until fragrant, about a minute. Add the curry powder, paprika, cumin and chili flakes. Stir well.

Add the chicken broth, tomatoes and cilantro. Simmer for about 15 minutes, until the sweet potatoes are softened and the chicken is cooked through.

Serve with cooked rice, extra chili flakes and cilantro.

TWEAK THE HEAT: If you want to REALLY up the heat factor of this dish, incorporate a ghost pepper into the mix. Ghost peppers are common in some Indian cooking, but beware, they are quite HOT. I once asked for a ghost pepper at an Indian restaurant and the owner said, "Are you sure?" He and the chef peeked around the corner as I ate it and couldn't believe it when I finished the plate. I do love it spicy!

Sticky Chinese-Style
CHICKEN WINGS
WITH HABANERO

Chicken wings are super easy to prepare, especially when they are baked. As much as I enjoy a good fried chicken wing, I prefer to bake them at home because cleanup is trouble-free. The hardest part is waiting for wings to come out of the oven.

2 lbs (907 g) chicken wings, separated and wing tips removed

1 tbsp (15 ml) sesame oil, plus 1 tsp, divided

1 tbsp (8 g) hot pepper flakes, plus 1 tsp, divided

Salt and pepper to taste

1–2 habanero peppers, chopped

1 tsp fresh chopped ginger

½ cup (120 ml) soy sauce

½ cup (160 g) honey

Fresh parsley, sesame seeds and ranch dressing or sour cream, for serving

Preheat the oven to 350°F (180°C). Pat the chicken wings down with a paper towel, then toss them in a bowl with a tablespoon (15 ml) of the sesame oil, a teaspoon of hot pepper flakes, salt and pepper.

Place the wings on a large, lightly oiled baking sheet and bake them for 60 minutes, or until they are cooked through and the skins are nice and crispy.

In a large bowl, combine the remaining sesame oil, habanero peppers, ginger, soy sauce, honey and remaining hot pepper flakes. Toss the wings in the sauce.

Garnish with fresh parsley and sesame seeds. Serve with ranch dressing or sour cream.

TWEAK THE HEAT: You'll definitely get a good level of heat from the fresh, chopped habanero peppers and hot pepper flakes combination. If you're looking to really kick these up a notch, include extra habanero peppers, or use a spicy chili powder in the seasoning. For a milder version, skip the habanero altogether or substitute it with a milder sweet pepper.

PREP TIME

5 minutes

COOKING TIME

60 minutes

SERVES

4

HEAT LEVEL

Hot

PREP
TIME

5 minutes

COOKING
TIME

15 minutes

SERVES

4

HEAT
LEVEL

Mild

Zesty Brazilian Fish and
SHRIMP STEW
(MOQUECA)

This is not a "hot" dish by any means, but WOW does it have a lot of flavor, and it is incredibly easy to make. It's a flavorful and fragrant mixture of coconut milk, fresh tomatoes, lime juice and light seasonings, with the seafood gently poached in the liquid. Palm oil is traditionally used, but I like to substitute it with coconut oil or olive oil, which is always on hand.

1 lb (454 g) firm white fish, cut into large pieces (I like halibut for this, but any firm white fish will do)

1 lb (454 g) shrimp, peeled and deveined

10 cloves garlic, minced, divided

Juice from 1 large lime, plus more for serving

Salt and pepper to taste

1 tbsp (15 ml) olive oil

1 medium sweet onion, chopped

1 large sweet pepper, chopped (bell pepper is fine)

2 large tomatoes, finely chopped (about 1½ cups [241 g])

1 tbsp (7 g) paprika

1 cup (240 ml) vegetable stock (or fish stock if you have it)

1 (14-oz [414-ml]) can coconut milk

2 tbsp (28 g) coconut oil (or olive oil)

2 tbsp (2 g) fresh chopped cilantro, plus more for garnish

2 tbsp (8 g) fresh chopped parsley, plus more for garnish

Cooked white rice and chili oil (optional), for serving

In a large bowl, add the fish and shrimp and toss them with half the garlic, lime juice, salt and pepper. Coat well.

In a large pot set to medium heat, add the olive oil. Add the onion and sweet pepper. Cook them down for about 5 minutes to soften. Add the remaining garlic and cook for another minute, until fragrant.

Add the tomatoes, paprika, stock, coconut milk and coconut oil and stir. Bring the pot to a quick boil, then reduce the heat and let it simmer for 5 minutes. Add a pinch of salt and pepper to taste, if desired.

Add the fish and shrimp, and let the pot simmer for about 5 minutes, or until the fish and shrimp are cooked through.

Stir in the cilantro and parsley, then serve in bowls with white rice, if desired. Garnish with extra parsley and cilantro. If you're using the chili oil, drizzle some over the top.

TWEAK THE HEAT: As mentioned, this recipe won't bring you much heat, but it really has a lot of flavor. If you're looking for a spicier version, you can easily incorporate spicy chili flakes, spicy curry or go with a hot chili oil for drizzling over the top of the dish.

The Zesty Sauce Project

I'm including a chapter here called "The Zesty Sauce Project" because it's something I've been doing for years that saves me a LOT of time during the busy week. I LOVE my spicy foods and big flavors, but it's hard sometimes to find time for cooking when the schedule fills up with work and other obligations. What I like to do is make a double or triple batch of a sauce or a chili paste, usually on a Sunday, which I can save in the refrigerator for use later in the week.

In some cases, you'll just use the same sauce, but sometimes I like to add a couple more ingredients to the sauce or paste to give myself a bit of variety. These recipes are some of my favorites, including some recipes to utilize them in.

PREP
TIME

5 minutes

COOKING
TIME

20 to 30
minutes

MAKES

about 2 cups
(450 g)

HEAT
LEVEL

Mild

Mexican "Holy Trinity"
CHILI PASTE

Chili pastes made from dried Mexican peppers offer a depth of flavor you won't find elsewhere. They are fundamental to many Mexican dishes, though I enjoy using them in non-traditional ways. Mexicans use a variety of dried peppers, but the "Holy Trinity" includes the ancho, mulato and pasilla peppers.

Anchos are dried, ripe poblano peppers and offer a complex fruity flavor. Mulato peppers are also dried poblanos, but have a smoky quality. Pasillas are dried chilaca peppers with a mild heat and rich flavor. Together they are used to make numerous traditional sauces and meals.

Fortunately for us, they're easy to use. Making chili pastes takes very little time, and you can keep a batch in the refrigerator for weeks. With a good chili paste on hand, you can whip together flavorful meals in very little time. If you have a hard time finding all these peppers, try making your paste from a single pepper.

4–5 dried ancho peppers
4–5 dried mulato peppers
3–4 dried pasilla peppers
2 tbsp (30 ml) olive oil, divided

1 small yellow onion, chopped
3–4 cloves garlic, chopped
Salt to taste

In a large pan set to medium-high heat, dry toast the dried ancho, mulato and pasilla peppers for about 30 to 60 seconds per side. The skins will start to puff up a bit and you'll notice the fragrance. This helps release the oils from the dried pods.

In a large bowl, add the toasted peppers and pour boiling water over them. Cover and let them sit for about 20 minutes to soften.

Remove them from the water and reserve the water. The water will be dark from the peppers and has plenty of nutrients. Cut the stems from the peppers. Slice them open and remove the seeds.

In a small pan, heat a tablespoon (15 ml) of the olive oil. Add the onion and cook for about 4 to 5 minutes to soften. Add the garlic and cook for a minute, stirring occasionally. Remove from the heat.

In the food processor, add the peppers, onion, garlic and a pinch of salt. Process to form a thick paste. Transfer to a container and top with the remaining olive oil. Cover and refrigerate. The paste should last for a couple of weeks.

TWEAK THE HEAT: You can add other seasonings to the paste, such as Mexican oregano, dried basil, cumin, ground cloves or other chili powders. I like to use this paste as my base, so I keep the ingredients to a minimum. They are still very big on flavor.

Chorizo and Potato
TORTAS—"PAMBAZOS"

We have a lot of Mexican restaurants in my town, but sadly, almost none of them serve pambazos—torta breads dipped in chili sauce, lightly fried and filled with a combination of potato and chorizo. They're easy to put together once you have a good paste on hand. Traditionally, they are made with guajillo sauce, but this version is just as delicious.

1 lb (454 g) yellow potatoes, quartered

¼ cup (55 g) Mexican "Holy Trinity" Chili Paste (page 162), or more to taste

1 (15-oz [425-g]) can tomato sauce

1 lb (454 g) Mexican chorizo (I use a spicy variety)

2 jalapeño peppers, chopped

2 tbsp (30 ml) olive oil

4 torta buns (bolillo buns are good, or any sturdy sandwich roll)

Shredded lettuce, sour cream or Mexican crema, hot sauce and crumbly white cheese, for serving

PREP TIME

10 minutes

COOKING TIME

15 to 20 minutes

SERVES

4

HEAT LEVEL

Medium-Hot

In a large pot, boil the potatoes in lightly salted water until soft, about 15 minutes. Drain and set them aside.

While the potatoes are boiling, heat a large pan to medium heat. Add the chili paste and tomato sauce. Mix well, then reduce the heat to simmer.

In a separate large pan, add the Mexican chorizo and jalapeño peppers. Cook them down for about 6 to 7 minutes, or until the chorizo is cooked through. Add the potatoes and roughly mash them into the chorizo mixture. Scoop the contents of the pan into a large bowl and return the pan to medium heat. Add in the olive oil.

Dip the torta buns into the tomato-chili sauce. Coat each side evenly. Set them into the other hot pan and lightly fry them on each side until they start to become crispy.

Slice open the buns and stuff them with the potato-chorizo mixture. Drizzle in some extra sauce. Serve with lettuce, sour cream or crema, hot sauce and crumbly white cheese.

TWEAK THE HEAT: You can enjoy a milder version of this recipe by omitting the jalapeño peppers and choosing a milder variety of Mexican chorizo. This is also great with refried beans and/or avocado.

Spicy Chicken Tortilla Soup

Most definitely a FAVE in our house. This soup brings in the flavors of tomatillos, fresh corn and a variety of peppers stewed with the magic of the Mexican "Holy Trinity" Chili Paste. The result is a big bowl of awesome flavor. I love this with fresh avocados and a bit of lime over the top.

PREP TIME

10 minutes

COOKING TIME

30 minutes

SERVES

4-6

HEAT LEVEL

Medium

1 tbsp (15 ml) olive oil

1 medium yellow onion, chopped

1 poblano pepper, chopped

1 serrano pepper, chopped

2 jalapeño peppers, chopped

2 cloves garlic, chopped

1½ lbs (681 g) tomatillos, peeled and chopped

¼ cup (55 g) Mexican "Holy Trinity" Chili Paste (page 162), or more to taste

1 [14-oz (397-g)] can tomato sauce

3-4 cups (720–960 ml) chicken broth

Corn from 3 ears (or use 1½ cups [216 g] frozen corn)

1 tsp paprika

½ tsp cumin

Salt and pepper to taste

½ cup (8 g) chopped cilantro, plus more for serving

Diced avocado, tortilla chips, crumbly white cheese and lime wedges, for serving

Heat a large pot to medium heat and add the olive oil. Add the onion, poblano, serrano and jalapeño peppers, and cook them down for about 5 minutes to soften them up. Add the garlic and cook for another minute, until fragrant.

Add the tomatillos and cook them down for about 5 minutes, until they release their juices.

Add the Mexican "Holy Trinity" Chili Paste, tomato sauce, chicken broth, corn, paprika, cumin, salt and pepper. Stir well. Let it simmer for 20 minutes to let the flavors develop. Adjust for salt and pepper.

Remove the pot from the heat and stir in the cilantro. Serve in bowls and top with avocado, tortilla chips, crumbly white cheese and chopped cilantro. Squeeze lime juice over the top.

HOT TIP: Use only 2 to 3 cups (480 to 720 ml) of chicken broth for a thicker version of this soup, or add up to 4 cups (960 ml) to stretch it out. Feel free to add in more of the Mexican "Holy Trinity" Chili Paste for a richer flavor.

TWEAK THE HEAT: Increase the heat factor by doubling up the amount of serrano peppers, or omit them for a milder version.

Chipotle—Honey—Tequila
BBQ SAUCE

A good BBQ sauce will last you through the week if you make a good-sized batch on Sunday. Just keep it in the refrigerator for quick and easy meals. This particular sauce is rather simple to make, as it is mostly about chopping and simmering. It is slightly sweet from the addition of honey, smoky with a good zing from the chipotles, and rich and complex from the añejo tequila. This is one of my favorite BBQ sauces.

1 tbsp (15 ml) olive oil
1 jalapeño pepper, chopped
2 serrano peppers, chopped
1 small yellow onion, chopped
2 tsp (6 g) fresh minced garlic
1 (7-oz [198-g]) can chipotle peppers in adobo sauce
6 oz (170 g) tomato paste
½ cup (120 ml) apple cider vinegar
½ cup (120 g) light brown sugar

6 tbsp (90 ml) Worcestershire sauce
⅓ cup (80 ml) añejo tequila
3 tbsp (60 g) honey
1 tsp cayenne powder
1 tsp paprika
1 tsp ancho chili powder
½ tsp cumin
1 tsp ground mustard
Salt and pepper to taste

PREP TIME

5 minutes

COOKING TIME

30 minutes

MAKES

2 cups (454 g)

HEAT LEVEL

Medium

Heat a large saucepan to medium heat and add the olive oil. Add the jalapeño, serranos and onion, and cook for 5 minutes to soften.

Add the garlic and cook for another minute, or until the garlic browns and becomes fragrant.

Add the chipotle peppers, tomato paste, vinegar, sugar, Worcestershire, tequila, honey, cayenne, paprika, chili powder, cumin, mustard, salt and pepper. Mix well. Bring the sauce to a quick boil, then reduce the heat to low. Simmer for about 20 minutes, stirring occasionally. The sauce will slightly thicken.

You can serve it like this, or you can add a bit of water to thin out the consistency. In a food processor, process until smooth.

TWEAK THE HEAT: You'll get a nice kick from the serrano peppers. If you're looking for a milder version, swap them out for more jalapeño peppers, which will still deliver a good heat factor. If you're looking to spice things up, add in hotter peppers, such as habaneros or 7-Pot peppers for an extra hot version. You can also add in more cayenne powder, which has a good heat level.

PREP
TIME

10 minutes

COOKING
TIME

30 minutes

SERVES

4

HEAT
LEVEL

Medium

BBQ Pulled Pork
MAC AND CHEESE WITH CRISPY JALAPEÑO COINS

This recipe always reminds me of summer, hanging out at our local "ribfest" every year, enjoying the local bands and eating all the great barbecue the competitors have to offer. I always get a plateful of BBQ pulled pork mac and cheese, slathered with a mixture of my favorite BBQ sauces. It's a bit decadent, but absolutely delicious, and super easy to put together when you have the sauce and pulled pork already made.

FOR THE MAC AND CHEESE

8 oz (227 g) prepared pulled pork (see recipe on page 130)

1 cup (225 g) Chipotle-Honey-Tequila BBQ Sauce (page 169), divided

2 cups (232 g) elbow macaroni noodles

1½ cups (195 g) shredded pepper Jack cheese

½ cup (115 g) goat cheese

Salt and pepper to taste

FOR THE JALAPEÑO COINS

2–3 cups (480–720 ml) peanut or vegetable oil (enough to cover the battered jalapeño peppers)

½ cup (62 g) all-purpose flour

½ tsp garlic powder

½ tsp paprika

Salt and pepper to taste

2 large eggs

3 jalapeño peppers, sliced into rings

Heat a small pan to low heat and add the pulled pork with about half of the BBQ sauce. Let it simmer while you prepare everything else.

In a medium pot, boil the noodles in lightly salted water according to the package instructions, about 10 minutes. Drain, then combine the pepper Jack cheese and goat cheese a bit at a time until they are nicely melted through. Season with salt and pepper.

While the noodles are cooking, heat the oil in a large pan to medium heat. Do not let it boil.

In a large mixing bowl, combine the flour, garlic powder, paprika and salt and pepper. Beat the eggs into the batter. In batches, coat the sliced jalapeño peppers in the batter.

Fry the battered peppers for a couple minutes each, turning if needed, until golden. Drain on paper towels.

To serve, pile the cheesy noodles into bowls. Add the BBQ pulled pork, then top with crispy jalapeño coins and the remaining BBQ sauce.

TWEAK THE HEAT: If you're looking for more of that heat factor, adjust your initial BBQ sauce with hotter peppers or hotter chili powders. I also like to incorporate ghost pepper powders, which I make each year from grinding dehydrated, home-grown ghost peppers.

Baked BBQ
CHICKEN WINGS

With your ready-made Chipotle-Honey-Tequila BBQ Sauce on hand, you can quickly bring a bit of zing to your chicken wings. No need to head out to your favorite wing joint when you can make these at home. Baking them is less messy than frying them, and requires very little work. Most of the work is waiting for them to be done!

PREP TIME

10 minutes

COOKING TIME

60 minutes

SERVES

4

HEAT LEVEL

Medium

2 lbs (907 g) chicken wings, separated and wing tips removed

1 tbsp (11 g) baking powder

1 tbsp (9 g) garlic powder

3 tbsp (27 g) chili powder

Salt and pepper to taste

1 cup (225 g) Chipotle-Honey-Tequila BBQ Sauce (page 169)

Fresh lime wedges, for serving

Pat the wings dry. This will help with the crispiness.

In a large bowl, add the wings and season with the baking powder, garlic powder, chili powder, salt and pepper. Toss well. The baking powder helps with the crispiness by drawing out the moisture.

Heat your oven to 250°F (120°C). Set the wings on a lightly oiled baking sheet and bake for 30 minutes.

Increase the oven heat to 425°F (220°C) and bake for 30 minutes, or until the wings are cooked through and the skins are crispy.

When the wings are nearly done, warm up the sauce in a pan for about 5 minutes.

In a large bowl, add the wings and pour the sauce over them. Toss well to coat.

Serve with lime wedges.

TWEAK THE HEAT: You can spice these wings up even more by including a spicy chili powder in your initial coating of the wings. I like to serve mine with chili pepper slices for a bit of added heat.

PREP
TIME

5 minutes

COOKING
TIME

15 minutes

MAKES

about
5-6 cups
(1.1-1.4 kg)

HEAT
LEVEL

Mild-Hot

Spicy Pineapple-Mango
PEPPER SAUCE

Bring a taste of the tropics to your kitchen! It is incredibly easy to prepare and you can make a large batch to use throughout the week for quick meals. You can use this basic sauce for marinating or spooning over grilled meats, or use it as a base to whip up some quick and easy spicy recipes.

1 cup (170 g) chopped chili peppers

1 large mango, peeled, cored and chopped (about 1 cup [165 g])

1 pineapple, peeled, cored and chopped (about 4 cups [660 g])

¼ cup (4 g) chopped cilantro

1 cup (240 ml) apple cider vinegar

¼ cup (60 ml) water, or more as needed

2 tbsp (40 g) honey

Salt to taste

In a food processor or blender, combine the chili peppers, mango, pineapple, cilantro, apple cider vinegar, water, honey and salt. Process until smooth.

In a pot or large pan, pour the sauce and bring to a quick boil. Reduce the heat and simmer for 15 minutes, stirring occasionally. Remove it from the heat and let it cool.

If you'd like the sauce a bit thinner, stir in a bit more water.

Transfer the sauce to a sealable container and refrigerate until ready to use. Because of the vinegar content, this sauce will keep in the fridge, covered, for a month or longer.

TWEAK THE HEAT: You can use sweet bell peppers for the mildest version of this recipe. For a very spicy version, go with Scotch bonnets, which are very popular with Caribbean cooking. You can also find a balance of heat by combining sweet peppers with 1 or 2 Scotch bonnets. If you'd like some "real" heat, make this with ghost peppers or other super hot chili peppers.

Spicy Pineapple-Mango
SHRIMP STIR-FRY

Having the Spicy Pineapple-Mango Pepper Sauce on hand adds a lot of extra flavor to your typical stir fry, as well as a blast of tropical flavor. Stir-fry dishes, in general, are quick and easy to make, and now they're even EASIER (and tastier) with this sauce.

2 tbsp (30 ml) olive oil

2–3 cups (340–510 g) chopped chili peppers

1 bunch asparagus, ends trimmed, roughly chopped

1 lb (454 g) shrimp, peeled and deveined

1 tbsp (7 g) smoked paprika

1 tsp garlic powder

Salt and pepper to taste

8 oz (227 g) cooked noodles

1 cup (225 g) Spicy Pineapple-Mango Pepper Sauce (page 174)

1 tbsp (14 g) gochujang

2 tbsp (28 g) chili-garlic sauce

Dash of Louisiana-style hot sauce

Sesame seeds, spicy chili flakes and sliced cherry tomatoes, for serving

PREP TIME

5 minutes

COOKING TIME

12 to 15 minutes

SERVES

4

HEAT LEVEL

Medium–Hot

Heat a large pan to medium-high heat and add the olive oil. Add the chili peppers and asparagus and cook, stirring often, for about 6 to 7 minutes. Set them aside.

Pat the shrimp dry, then season them with the paprika, garlic, salt and pepper. Add the shrimp to the pan (you might need to add a bit more oil) and cook them for a couple minutes per side, or until they are nicely cooked through. Add the cooked peppers, asparagus and noodles.

In a small mixing bowl, combine the Spicy Pineapple-Mango Pepper Sauce, gochujang, chili-garlic sauce and hot sauce. Pour it into the pan and stir well. Make sure to coat the shrimp evenly.

Remove from the heat and serve in bowls topped with sesame seeds, chili flakes and sliced cherry tomatoes.

HOT TIP: I like to change up the types of peppers used when making stir-fry dishes. I'll often just toss in what I've picked up at the store or whatever I've grown in the garden that year. For this particular dish, I used an orange bell pepper, some shishitos, a couple small spicy red peppers and an Anaheim, so it wasn't overly spicy.

TWEAK THE HEAT: You can easily spice things up with a habanero or Scotch bonnet here.

PREP
TIME

10 minutes

COOKING
TIME

25 minutes

SERVES

4

HEAT
LEVEL

Medium-Hot

Caribbean-Style Salmon
WITH COCONUT-PINEAPPLE-MANGO RICE

With your handy Spicy Pineapple-Mango Pepper Sauce at the ready, you can whip up Caribbean-flavored dishes in no time. I'm a huge fan of salmon and love to pan sear it for a nice, crispy skin, but this recipe will work just as great for a nice white fish fillet, such as mahi mahi, grouper or wahoo.

FOR THE COCONUT-PINEAPPLE-MANGO RICE

2 cups (421 g) white rice

1 (13.5-oz [398-ml]) can coconut milk

1½ cups (360 ml) water

Salt and pepper to taste

½ cup (85 g) chopped spicy peppers, or more to your preference

1 cup (225 g) Spicy Pineapple-Mango Pepper Sauce (page 174), plus more for serving

1 tbsp (4 g) fresh chopped parsley, plus more for serving

FOR THE SALMON

4 (6-oz [170-g]) salmon fillets, skin on

1 tbsp (7 g) paprika

1 tbsp (9 g) garlic powder

Salt and pepper to taste

2 tbsp (30 ml) olive oil

Cooked white rice and spicy chili flakes, for serving

In a large pot, combine the rice, coconut milk, water, salt and pepper. Bring the mix to a boil, then reduce the heat to low. Add the spicy chopped peppers and cover the pot. Simmer for 20 minutes.

Remove the lid and cook for 5 minutes, or until all of the liquid is absorbed and the rice is fluffy. Stir in the Spicy Pineapple-Mango Pepper Sauce and chopped parsley.

For the salmon, pat each fillet dry with a paper towel. This will help make the skin crispy. Season each fillet with paprika, garlic, salt and pepper. Heat a large cast iron pan to medium-high heat and heat the olive oil through.

Add the salmon one fillet at a time, skin-side down. Each time, press the salmon to the bottom of the pan so that the skins stick and don't curl up, about 10 seconds each. Cook them for about 5 minutes each, then carefully lift them with a spatula. If the skin sticks, lift them gently at the edges until the skins loosen. Flip the fillets and cook them for 1 or 2 minutes, until the center is rare, or a few minutes longer if you prefer your salmon more medium.

Serve the salmon fillets on rice. Drizzle on extra Spicy Pineapple-Mango Pepper Sauce, spicy chili flakes and fresh chopped parsley.

HOT TIP: I enjoy my salmon with a rare interior, which is 110°F (43°C) internally, though you can easily cook them a bit longer to your preference.

SPICY FOOD LOVERS' SECRET WEAPONS

If you want to cook up spicy food, you need the proper ingredients. Aside from all of the amazing spices available to you, consider using the freshest produce available, as well as investigating the growing world of spicy condiments and hot sauces. If you have a well-stocked pantry, you can create satisfying, spicy meals in an hour or less, most in 30 minutes or less.

The following is not an exhaustive list of items, but ingredients that I cook with quite often. Almost all of them appear in the book in some way. I try to keep as many of these on hand at all times for my own general cooking. What can I say? I love it spicy!

BUFFALO SAUCE: An American classic, it's a mixture of hot sauce and butter with a bit of tangy vinegar. Most people associate it with chicken wings, which is GREAT! But, you can use it for so much more.

CHILI-GARLIC SAUCE: A hot and tangy blend of chili peppers and garlic, perfect for adding punch and brightness to your dishes.

CHILI OIL: Usually made with neutral cooking oil, like vegetable oil, though you can find olive oils, infused with chili peppers. They are great for sautéing, but ideal for layering flavor into food as you cook, primarily as a finisher. I love my chili oils, but I also recommend other infused oils, such as garlic oil or truffle oil.

CHIPOTLE IN ADOBO AND CHIPOTLE SAUCE: Great for adding zing to a variety of sauces and soups.

HOT GIARDINIERA: A Chicago must! It's mostly a finisher, but I like to add a jar into a slow cooker with a nice rump roast. Delish!

HOT SAUCE: This goes without saying! Hot sauces are typically finishing ingredients, but they really are great for layering into soups, stews, braising liquids, wet rubs and more. They're also great for making new sauces. It just depends on the type you're using. There is a HUGE variety out there to choose from. I dare you to try them all!

GOCHUJANG: This is a Korean chili paste that is gaining much popularity as of late. It's one of my favorites. If you can't find it, sriracha is a good substitute, though it isn't the same. Gochujang is much thicker and more condensed, perfect for mixing into sauces, soups, stews and so much more, without the sweet quality some srirachas offer.

HARISSA: A popular chili paste used in North African and Middle Eastern cuisine. The recipe varies by the region depending on the local ingredients, so you will find many variations. I have seen it made with tomatoes, mint, different types of chili peppers and more. I often like to toss in some lightly roasted habanero peppers or maybe even a superhot or two when I make my homemade version.

PEPPER JAM: Perfect for glazes or finishing grilled meats. They can range from sweet to spicy.

PICKLED PEPPERS: These offer a sweet and spicy crunch when you use them as a garnish, like topping a sandwich. You can also chop them and add them to soups, stews and more.

PREPARED HORSERADISH: Horseradish brings its characteristic ZING to your meals like nothing else can. Sure, it's great in that Bloody Mary, but it really shines in food.

SAMBAL OELEK: A classic chili paste used for cooking, made with a variety of ground chili peppers, vinegar and salt. It is ideal for seasoning noodle dishes and enhancing the flavors of sauces.

SPICY MUSTARD: Yellow mustard has its place, but a good spicy mustard, particularly a hot mustard or a spicy brown mustard, will add depth to your spicy dishes. I use it more as a component in the preparation than as a finisher.

SRIRACHA: Sriracha has taken America by storm so hard that it's practically replaced ketchup as the top condiment. In my world, it already has. There are different varieties out there with different flavor variations, so be sure to try a few and find your favorite. It's great for mixing new sauces and glazes.

THAI CHILI PASTE: Should be easy to find at your local grocer. It's a thick paste that can be swirled into stir-fry dishes and so much more.

THAI CHILI SAUCE: A great way to blend in flavor, not just for Thai cuisine, but for any cuisine.

ACKNOWLEDGMENTS

A special thanks to everyone at Page Street Publishing. I appreciate your working with me! You have been outstanding to work with.

I would also like to thank everyone who has ever visited my food blog, Chili Pepper Madness. You've all been great to hang with. You are the best people in the world!

I would like to, once again, acknowledge my wife, Patty (though she's still also Crazy Patty and always will be), for everything she's done in my life and for this book. She is integral to all of my efforts, and without her, this book and our website, www.chilipeppermadness.com, would only be a shadow of what it is. She truly rocks.

ABOUT THE AUTHOR

Michael Hultquist is the creator of Chili Pepper Madness, a food blog dedicated to creative yet approachable cooking with zesty food and big, bold flavors. His focus is on home cooking from scratch and bringing a bit of fun and spice to everyday meals. He is also the author of *The Spicy Dehydrator Cookbook*.

Check out the site at www.chilipeppermadness.com.

Mike is also a fiction author and produced screenwriter. You can learn more about Mike's works at www.michaelhultquist.com.

INDEX